ONE STAYED, ONE LEFT:

Choices Made by Two Gay Family Men

———

A Memoir

by

Lynn

Dedication

———

To

Uncle Art (1898-1983)

One who found The Answer (and the passion) in fragments

in the village of Cornucopia.

———

"Hey, Nephew! Down here! What a life they had planned for me! No, thank you!"

Contents on the Table

———

———

Intro

Needed: Proper shoes, laced up

———

We will be making "tracks" today, so, let's turn first to the experts on definitions. *Webster's New World Dictionary, Third College Edition* provides several descriptions.

Tracks . . . "to follow a track or footprints; to follow a path; to trace by means of evidence; to plot the path and collect data; to leave in the form of tracks."

There, that should do it. Now, please take my hand and allow me to introduce myself to you and, perhaps, with any luck, to yourself, all through tracking.

Let's get started.

Whether we know it or not, we are always looking for tracks. We search for tracks, we're on the lookout for tracks, we step in tracks to see if our foot fits or to see where the tracks lead.

Tracks can be hidden under leaves; it just takes a Tracker to find them. My brother, Rex Arthur, the hunter, made plaster of Paris castings of creature tracks, stored for many years in an old chest of drawers. (He could track, kill and skin expertly).

Tracks can be words; tracks can be gestures; lines from a play. Just to hear Maggie Smith simply say, "Life," can be life-saving.

Our own tracks are the important ones; they don't back down, they don't follow, they lead; lead in the way some birds know their destination over thousands of miles.

So, brave Tracker, I invite you to step into my tracks, all twelve of them. The letters speak for Jim. You will find me there, too, of course, hidden in plain sight. (I do wonder where my letters to him are.)

Trust me, these tracks will arrive at our destination. We'll be weary, but it is a place, a place called *home*.

———

King of the World
(A very short reign . . .)
Age 8

~~~~~

No, I was not a changeling!

Rather, I was of royal blood---a King---placed with an ordinary family, anticipating that one day I would be visited by crimson-robed courtiers in my middle-class home. In my bedroom, I would be dressed ceremoniously and taken to my rightful home; a palace, of course!

Well, needless to say, that didn't happen. I waited and waited, mainly at night in my bedroom, for my arrival and liberation.

The fantasy/belief ended one night with a shock. There were footfalls in the hallway! Excited, I sat straight up in the bed, ready to take my rightful place, at last! The soft sounds, alas, turned---it was my parents going into their bedroom!

At that devastating moment, I gave up my hopes and dreams. Now I must face my far less grand and powerless position. I must accept the fact that I shared a room with my older brother; he in the twin bed across the room. The night before, he had sent a slipper flying at me. "Turn out the light!" he yelled, interrupting my dreams.

Yes, there was a king in that bedroom, but it wasn't me! It was he with the kingly name - Rex Arthur!

Awakening
Age 14

~~~~~

It was the summer of 1948.

I was fourteen and joining my friends at the annual Methodist church camp on Lake Tahoe, in northern California. The camp itself was a large, imposing, rustic lodge built in the 1930s in a pine forest. The campers came from churches all over the northern part of the state.

One evening, the teens gathered for a walk. We were to go with candles down a path in the woods, stopping at stations of the cross. When we were asked to choose a partner, a handsome, curly-haired, blue-eyed boy approached me, smiled, and took my hand. I did not resist.

It was the first time I had held a boy's hand. I can still feel the warmth, the strength of it. We walked hand-in-hand, taking in the fragrance of the pines in the moist night air; the quiet peace of the woods. We walked in a certain natural rhythm, moving as one along the path, sharing each candle-lit station.

I was walking with a boy---and holding hands! Did he feel what I felt? Did he see what I saw? The dance continued to the trail's end. Were we the only ones on the path?

No act of love-making compares with the holding of hands. At fourteen, I had no comparison, but I stand with that thought today; the clasp follows the electric touch of one's skin touching another's; warm, muscular, encompassing, protective, caring; most importantly, *relaxing* and the feeling of *home*, at last.

I can feel his presence even now. I can feel the power of his soft affection and protection; his obvious caring about me, moment by moment. It was something that I had not felt before.

By the end of the trail that night, I was a different person---awakened and deeply *relaxed*; this joy, this life, and this was only the beginning . . .

The hands unclasped, but decades later, the spell remains unbroken.

I relive it now as an old man. What a gift.

~~~~~

Dear companion, sharing a walk in the woods,

I thank you, and clearly hope---*trust*---that other hands you have clasped have joined you on another path just as perfect as that one was to me.

~~~~~

Dancing Through the Tears
Ages 14-18

~~~~~

Dancing! Dancing everywhere!!

I loved to dance! With grammar school, it was folk dancing; with high school,

sock hops! I even danced in the aisles at our movie house with Betty, Eleanor, Ann and

Judy! Dancing, while my brother sank deeper into his seat out of embarrassment! But,

best of all, perhaps, I showed off at high school proms, all eight of them!

My best partner was Pat, a beautiful, five-foot, six-inch, sister-like neighbor who

could really *dance* and follow. And follow she did---everything I came up with---

whirling, dipping, spinning and traveling! We could circle the floor and never collide!

Pure joy! And, in my mind, the room would be filled with cheers---silent cheers!

But the joy would stop too often when I would suddenly tear up. It happened

often enough for Pat to put her figurative foot down and say, "Stop it or I'll leave the

floor!" My tears would stop then, but not the whirling.

The tears I eventually understood. In the midst of my happiness, I was

surrounded by straight guys with their dates. It created the feeling in me of being an

outsider and the knowledge that the joy I felt would always be limited. Sometimes, the feelings were just flashes, but they were enough. In the midst of the cheering, I realized

that I would never be able to do this joyful thing with the person I loved.

At sixteen, I knew that my life was going to be different. . . .

Yet another kind of awakening.

~~~~~

Facing the Implications
Age 17

~~~~~

The year was 1951.

I was a high-school senior and had always been drawn to the stage, appearing in twelve plays in four years. The play, this time, was "Our Town," by Thornton Wilder. I played seventeen-year-old George. He was in love with Emily.

In one scene, two tall ladders were placed opposite each other to create the illusion of George and Emily's corresponding bedroom windows as they talked with each other from house to neighboring house. I will never forget how it felt to be in that scene---hormones raging at seventeen---the story of George loving Emily. It was yet another situation where I *felt* the love story, but it emphasized my personal situation, squaring the "usual" or "normal" with what was a scary reality for me.

Nevertheless, the scene was atmospheric, simple but powerful---audiences cheered!

Still, it was an early example---a never-to-be-forgotten memory---of my being somebody else, and set me up for a lifetime of deception and tension. The so-called "*relaxation*" I had once felt vanished.

The play's setting was "Grover's Corners," a small town set in 1901; *my* town; *every* American town. In reality, "homos" did not exist in those towns.

Where was I to turn for models? To whom could I turn for understanding?

There was no one.

~~~~~

Summer Work ~ 1952-1956
Ages 18 - 22

~~~~~

Grizzly Creek Redwoods State Park was a campground setting among an awe-inspiring forest of old-growth redwood trees. For five summers, I was what was called a "park aide." I camped there all summer, built campfires, roasted marshmallows, entertained with sing-a-longs. and generally kept the camp presentable.

Most campers were well-kitted-out tent campers. There were lovely setups under the alders and towering redwoods, not far from the lazy Van Duzen River.

One day, while making my rounds, picking up litter with a pointed stick, I happened to glance into the camp of some new arrivals. Two men relaxed within. One of them was busy at a camp table; both were handsome and smiling.

One of them, his mate---(yes, I knew in an instant - *his mate*)---came out of the tent and saw me staring, (an unfortunate habit of mine), at the tableau. Two men comfortable at home; it was amazing to me! As I stood, motionless, the fellow at the tent saw me. Suddenly, he looked combative. The mood was broken. I came to myself and hurried on.

Lying on my cot that night, I pieced together the meaning of what I had seen.

I was over the moon, exhilarated---a gay couple camping like everybody else, one beautifully relaxed, the other *warning* me!

Hmm . . . gender roles . . . just like Mom and Dad . . .

The question it raised for me was profound: *What makes a home a home, and who is allowed inside?*

The choices were a man like my Uncle Art or the man who just couldn't seem to find the right woman. The search for a third choice, though I didn't know it then, had begun.

~~~~~

Jon's Letter
Age 20

~~~~~

The letters arrived almost daily that summer of 1954. I was twenty and had met the writer, Jon, in the early days of my sophomore year at San Francisco State the previous year. We fell in love and shared a wonderful, exciting year in that romantic city.

I sat reading his last letter, as it turned out to be, on a beautiful summer's day in the living room of my home.

Just as I came to the usual "I love you" closing the letter, I heard a gasp. My mother had been standing behind my chair, quietly reading over my shoulder.

Well, all hell broke loose. Daddy was told that night after work.

We three sat together there for several hours. Mother was never at a loss for words; Daddy looked miserable. I was tight-lipped until finally saying, "I think you fall in love like this once in a lifetime." (I was right).

I stood my ground for the next thirty-six hours. Mother was ready that second morning. She came into the breakfast room, silent for once. When she found her voice, what a message! It was a threat---*Leave him or I'll kill myself!* Daddy shot her a look.

I jumped up , went into the bathroom and sobbed. Some minutes later, I joined my parents and uttered those life-changing words: "I'll write to him and tell him it is over."

Mother had "won," but at what price? I never again had a full night's sleep.

When love walks in, hang on . . . for fear waits at the door.

Alas, I did not keep his beautiful letters. Letters, what treasures! Placed in a story, as I am now doing some sixty-five years later, those two love letters would be book-ends to a long life in words on paper.

What would the title be of the story of first love at age twenty? Of course, "The Answer," a story by Guy de Maupassant. (You'll find my college paper and *my* answer at the end of the *Tracks*).

~~~~~

TRACK #7

The Alarming of Sidney Armer
Age 24

~~~~~

The most beautiful garden in our town was graced by a Tudor-style house, the grounds leading down to a creek and the city park.

Sidney and Laura Armer, an extraordinary couple, moved there in 1945. They ended up changing my life.

Our first encounter happened when I was twelve or thirteen. I had passed the house many times on my way to the foot bridge to the park. One day, as I was coming home from the park, I couldn't contain my yearning to see the garden. I slipped in at the edge of it unnoticed, I thought, and it was lovely. But I had been seen. I hurried out, followed by the gardener and Mrs. Armer, as she glared at me!

Later, following idle conversations in the garden, the ice was broken and I entered their front door as a friend. There were wonderful visits, and in 1959, our wedding reception was to take place in their garden.

A few weeks before the ceremony, I went there alone to ask Sidney, who was aged ninety by then, a question. Marriage for me was risky, I knew, but I so cared for my fiancée that, at that moment, I believed that it was right. Yet, I must seek the answer to a question from the person whom I trusted and had turned to for so long. I knew the

Hallmark version of love and I wanted so much to lead a conventional life. But that wasn't what I needed at that moment. Sidney Armer was a person of vast experience, who cared about me. I had been his student in a dozen ways and at this juncture, I wanted his input, which, I knew, would be the unvarnished truth.

I sat there in his living room, staring into the fire, feeling the warmth I had felt countless times before, and asked my question: "How important is love in a marriage?" I'll never forget his reaction. He answered with his entire body: "*It is everything.*"

I couldn't move from the chair; the warmth of the fire couldn't dissolve the cold shiver of what I was feeling.

~~~~~

Two Weddings ~ One Summer
Age 25

~~~~~

Neighbor/dance partner/piano accompanist/friend Joy and I both got married during the summer of 1959. Same church, same minister, same guests, same organist. But that is where the similarities ended.

Joy's love, I'm sure, had grown day-by-day, so when that June day arrived, she and Joel were poised to move seamlessly into what was to be a sixty-year union.

Two months later, the situation was very different. I had found somebody I knew would help me bring to life my dream of being a father and having a conventional married life---and I loved and admired her.

I knew she would be an excellent mother and companion. But . . . how? Things progressed and I gradually became more and more confident, enough for me to feel I could do my part in every way.

Everyone was smiling, but what was behind those smiles? My father thinking, perhaps, of his gay brother; my mother's ear-to-ear smile, but why not? She had won with the full support of my slipper-throwing brother, who, I found out later, had threatened Jon with arrest for corrupting a minor! Far from it; I was *home*.

So, the weeks passed; invitations were mailed, church and music arrangements were made, and the reception planned at the Armer's lovely garden.

We were happy and I was over the moon until one evening, saying goodnight, I was aroused. I pushed her hand down, and she jumped back and screamed! As it turned out, this incident affected our entire married life and my own physical reactions; from then on, I knew something had happened to change things between us. I was panicked. She felt something, as she told me years later, had stopped my affection. (Her mother had told her to "save herself" until marriage).

Today's gay men would have called it off if it had gotten that far, but no, not me! I laid plans for suicide; the "accident" would involve a drowning.

So, when I walked down the aisle at the end of the ceremony in August, smiling---Joy sat in the pew this time, smiling---no one knew, except perhaps Sidney Armer, that all was not well.

There were difficult decisions to come, and the end of relaxation and sleep for me, if not the end of my life.

~~~~~

The Little White Book
Age 35

~~~~~

Litter bothers me. I've had a life of bending over, picking it up and throwing it away.

One day, a piece of litter---a plain, white matchbook---was lying on the sidewalk in front of me. As I reached for it, I had no idea that that act was going to dramatically change my life.

I had no history with match books; never smoked, but there it was; a tiny, white paper object with matches inside. I opened it and found an ad for a Berkeley bath house.

I wasn't quite sure what a bath house was, but those two words sent my mind to doing flip-flops. Was this little book meant for someone like me? I closed the book, crammed it in my pocket and my mind began to have new, exciting thoughts as I laid awake at 3:00 a.m.

Fantasy began filling in those hours; more and more hours, until there were times when I would go to work with only thirty minutes of sleep.

Let me say now that I took our wedding vows to heart and not once in seventeen years did I let those thoughts lead me to actions.

But, oh, those thoughts! The cracks in the dam got wider and wider until the floods swept through, devastating all of the structures we had built so carefully.

And, slowly, I began to drown.

~~~~~

Meeting Jim
Age 44

~~~~~

Frames---our walls are covered with them---framed landscapes, documents, photos. Frames protect, add importance and surround objects of our love.

I first saw Jim, standing framed in the doorway leading to a meeting of the Gay Fathers. He was there for the first time; I was a regular.

His impact on me at that moment created a top-to-bottom, weak-kneed, swooning, stammering mess. He was handsome, curly-headed, tall, sturdy, carelessly dressed, and when he finally *moved*, all was lost.

It can't be true, but I guess <u>love</u>---oh, that word, what a trap!---but, alas, I did indeed walk, weakly, right into . . . "it."

I cannot tell how long the meeting was, but his voice---assured, lip-smacking masculinity---*and* his story---left me wanting more and more. I got it.

He was on a six-month sabbatical from a mid-western university, married and father of two little girls.*

So, we fell, collided, collapsed into each other's arms. Joyous weeks followed in one of our most romantic and fascinating cities, San Francisco. Six months of no responsibilities, picnics, candle-lit dinners, hikes, ferry rides, parties and *the love-making-*

--at times we were more like two drowning people.

I came from a marriage that you, dear travelers, have read about in earlier tracks.

He was, at forty, the experienced one. I was an eager forty-four-year-old, six--foot,

uninitiated body ready to learn the gay ways.

To be fair, Jim might say something different; passion has its own built-in

learning track. He told me that those months were the happiest of his life; I said the

same.

By the end of our time (what a limited word!) together, we were sure. So, help

me finish that thought by continuing to read the letters and following the tracks.

* Flashing yellow light ignored.

~~~~~

LETTERS: Homoerotic Love While Parenting

Letter #1 - August 15, 1978

Dearest Lynn…

I love you, still and always. I think of you every day.
So, why haven't I written, you ask?

Little John's timing was perfect to illustrate my answer.
I just let in a friend of Emma's and they are now giggling and
getting reacquainted. So, my answer is if it isn't one thing,
then it's another. And I procrastinate, I admit. I think that
there is so much catching up to do, I will have to set aside a
couple of hours to write; just recollected my papers which a
wind has been scattering. If it isn't one thing, it's another.
I can't complain about the wind. It is the one relief we have
from this incessant and cloying humidity.

We are all finally moved back in, although I see there is
still a little clutter around the attic door. Sally is off at
her office, the kids are in their playroom; they play and
fantasize so well, now that they have been weaned off TV, that I
have decided not to subscribe to the cable service. I am
sitting up in our study loft, feet up on the desk, just a pair
of shorts on. We have a lake with a beach just a couple of
hundred yards from the house and I have been swimming across it
a couple of times a day. I thought it was ideal until yesterday
evening, when I noticed clusters of itchy bumps on my scalp and
more than the usual number of "mosquito bites", elsewhere. It
is "swimmer's itch". When the water warms up, and it is perfect
now, a parasite on ducks comes to live there. If you let the
water dry on you when you come out, the parasite burrows into
your skin. It finds out, however, that you are not a duck. So,
it dies. In the meantime, you itch.

But I had my gay hairdresser give me a real scratch of a shampoo. The scratchy brush was also quite satisfying. In the meantime, we sniffed each other out, naming places and that sort of thing. Finally, toward the end, I found a way to casually come out to him. And that's just where it stands. But it's a beginning.

I gave him some hints. Do you think my naval uniform would make him suspect? Incidentally, I dropped my suspenders. No, you silly. I have ceased wearing them. They are too short, which does wonders for crotch visibility but is really agonizing. Anyway, I have noticed that baskets become much more subtle, as one travels east.

Suspenders may become part of the macho look. I attended the lumberman jamboree in North Fork, near Bass Lake. The lumberjocks wore suspenders...especially the younger ones (or maybe I was just paying attention to the younger ones). No earrings, however. When I was in the Black Hills, South Dakota, I toured a gold mine and saw a miner with suspenders. So, if they're on the macho hard hat traders, Castro Street won't be far behind. But I also attended a rodeo in Salt Lake City and found no suspenders at all. So, they won't become part of the cowboy look.

In Yosemite, which you must condescend to visit sometime, I fell in love with the stars and got myself a book that, long last, made it possible for me to recognize the constellations. I learned all the July sky constellations; Hercules still gives me trouble but the rest I can SEE. I don't know how many times I have tried to learn but I have always failed. I think my success is due to the book, which I now recommend as a must for school libraries. It is:

H.A. Rey - *The Stars: A New Way to See Them*, Enlarged World Wide Edition; Houghton Mifflin Co.;

Paperback $5.95.

Now, my fun is to discover, each month, the new
constellations that become visible in the eastern sky. I almost
feel that there are certain emotions you get from gazing at the
different constellations. My favorite is Cygnus the Swan,
flying south along the Milky Way. I also love to gaze at Lyra,
which to me looks like a butterfly or moth. Then, there is
spectacular Scorpio, with his claws sticking up out of the
southern sky. Right now, there is a meteor shower coming out of
Perseus but I cannot brave the mosquitoes; will have to wait
until after the first frost to renew my stargazing.

We tented through seven national parks (Yosemite, Zion,
Grand Canyon – north rim, Bryce, Yellowstone, Grand Tetons, Wind
Cave) and seven national monuments (Pinnacles, Death Valley,
Craters of the Moon, Timpanogos Cove, Jewel Cave, Mount
Rushmore, and Devil's Tower - no landings were scheduled that
night) and national forests, state parks, six weeks on the road
and only five nights in motels. I found three inches of foam
rubber and a sleeping bag perfectly comfortable. But when we
went to motels, I couldn't sleep!

The best place we stayed at was The Old Faithful Inn, in
Yellowstone. It is an incredibly interesting old Victorian
building. We somehow got the only room in the building that had
both a view of Old Faithful to one side and a view of the main
geyser field to the other. It was our cheapest night, too:
twenty dollars.

(Back from getting kids wagon and a bite to eat.) I lost
five pounds on the trip. I can't imagine where from; certainly
not my belly. That's still there. I think I must have lost 5
pounds of muscle and bone.

If you are interested in any of the parks I saw, let me
know and I'll go into detail. You should not allow yourself to

be "Jarvis Ganned" out of a vacation. For less than fifteen
dollars, you can get three inches foam rubber pad and tour the
parks. No need to bother with motels. As for food, a Coleman
stove and two dollars of gas will last...

That was John's mother...if it ain't one thing, etc.,
etc...will last two weeks. Let's see...fourteen cans of
asparagus soup - seven dollars, two dollars gas, and all the
grass you can eat, free. That comes to...seriously, we have our
own Jarvis Gann coming up in November: the Tisch Amendment.

And that was the president of our union chapter on the
phone. If it ain't, etc., etc. I got drunk with him, last
weekend. What a god-awful combination: first scotch until that
ran out, then bourbon. I skipped the tequila, which was next.
Then, Gallo burgundy, then rose. By that time, it was 2:00AM.
But it was a fine homecoming and reunion with my union cronies.
The next morning, I was still dizzy, took a glass of orange
juice, threw that up...not the liquor, just the good orange
juice, mind you...and went back to bed. Around 3, I ate my
breakfast waffles Sally had made.

We have gorged ourselves on blueberries: blueberry pie,
blueberry muffins, blueberry crumb cake, blueberry pancakes,
blueberry waffles. We picked eleven pounds of them (sixty cents
a pound!). The kids fancy themselves as bakers. Sally is
reveling in the farmers market here, also. Twice a week, there
are about 100 farmer stalls filled with produce galore. You
would go mad! Your salads would rival Everest. There's now a
variety of yellow corn that is extra sweet. I couldn't believe
it. And flowers! We have bouquets all over.

I'm going to sign off, my sweetest. I have jacked off
thinking of you. And I feel a more-than-a-little hardening as I
remember our wonderful lovemaking. Maybe when I get a PO box,
we can write jack off letters to one another. Do you think we

could make love by mail? Make mail love, male love. By now,
you have a lover, right?

I have enjoyed writing this chatty, rambling letter to you.
It is almost like the rambling we did over asparagus soup in
between our prolonged passion-swollen kissing. I will write
again, if you don't mind a mind wandering on paper.

And say hello for me to your two charming chicken delights.
Incidentally, I am not much on military things, but I was
enriched emotionally, as well as intellectually, by the museum
at the spot where Custer made his last stand. It was
scrupulously fair, unflinchingly honest about Indian-White
relations, very informative about the actual battle. If Kit is
ever in eastern Wyoming, he would love to visit it, I'm sure.

Love and kisses...Jim

Love's Philosophy

The fountains mingle with the river
    And the rivers with the ocean;
The winds of heaven mix forever
    With a sweet emotion;

Nothing in the world is single;
    All things by a law divine
In one another's being mingle---
    Why not I with thine?

See the mountains kiss high heaven,
    And the waves clasp one another;
No sister-flower would be forgiven
    If it disdain'd its brother;
And the sunlight clasps the earth,
    And the moonbeams kiss the sea---
What are all these kissings worth,
    If thou kiss not me?

~ Percy Bysshe Shelley (1792-1822)

Letter #2 - September 20, 1978

Dearest...

At last! Don't scold me for not writing sooner; I feel guilty enough, already. First, <u>all</u> four grandparents visited us, and my brother. The last set of grandparents took off a little over a week ago. And I've given birth to another paper; short one, this time.

Your letters are a breath of fresh air to me. It's claustrophobic in here, in the closet. I liked the story about Anita being a latent alcoholic, etc., etc. Incidentally, I even saw a car go by with a "Support ERA" sticker on one end of the bumper and a "Boycott Florida Oranges" on the other end. Handsome stud at the wheel, too. Right here in lil' 'ol middle America! It was the only such stickers I've seen, however.

My gay activity is still zilch. However, I am planning to go to a convention, ha-ha, and will stay overnight with a fellow...a librarian, wouldn't you know...who I met through an *Advocate* ad. He was married at the time but is now divorced. He's a come down from you, of course, but he's a cum. Besides, I will have built up 3½ months of horniness, by then. My hairdresser, John...he calls himself Jonathan but the certificate on the wall says "John"...I haven't seen him again but I'll make an appointment for next week. Perhaps he also gives massages; I'll ask.

I went to the post office to ask about the box. But I got cold feet when the lady announced that my signature would have to be verified by my local carrier. I began to imagine scenes like him ringing the bell and telling Sally that her husband's PO Box application has been approved.

Which reminds me of jack off letters. Shortly after classes began, this black stud with beautiful Polynesian-type eyes, walks into my office. Here I am, horny as all get out from looking over the latest crop. I had noticed, however, that baskets are not as explicit as they are on the streets of San Francisco. No tubular projections down the pant legs. This Polynesian walks into my office and gives me a beautiful smile and I naturally look over his muscular arms and chest, the shirt being open. But my heart just leapt when I got down to his stuff. There was one of the thickest and longest tubular projections I've ever seen! I just stared. He had cut-off jeans and I wondered if I could scrunch down in my chair enough to look up into them and see that marvelous corona. You could see the ring of his corona.

In the meantime, he is asking if he can add my class and I am saying yes and getting up to get the form and handing it to him to fill out. But he saw my staring and his smile got bigger. He tossed his head as he talked and lifted his shirt off his torso, ostensibly to scratch his side but really to let me see more. My heart was pounding. I was on the verge of saying something. There was something in his manner that was egging me on.

"That's a great basket you have there," I said, as he was filling out the forms. It was out of my mouth before I could think about it. He looked at me with a puzzled look, and I was about to jump out the window but instead, I just put on a casual smile and pointedly stared at his basket.

Suddenly, he lights up with understanding and says, "Oh, you mean this?", and he puts his long slender fingers on his long tubular projection and begins slowly stroking it with a hearty laugh. Obviously, this fellow has no sexual hang-ups.

I laugh, too. Just think...a second ago, I was going to jump out the window. Then, I get up and shut my office door and he gives out a knowing giggle. "Let me do that stroking for you and you can finish filling out the forms." "All right," he says in a long, drawn out sing-songy way and I put my hand on that long tubular projection. It was thick and the head on it was just marvelous. I probed gently around the base of the corona and he gave an appreciative moan, as he filled out the forms.

I was feeling much more at ease, now. Cock is my pacifier. And his cock was growing in response to my caresses. And sure enough, it emerged from the bottom of his cut-offs.

I got down on my knees and gave that big tip some tongue action and that stud gave out another moan. So, I unzipped his pants and just pulled them down. (I could never get that cock back up that pant leg.) He had beautiful thighs and a perfect groin and great ass. I decided this was going to be all the way, right then and there...and so did he. He put his forms down, put his hands on my shoulders, and got ready for some real sucking action. I took that pecker all the way in just to measure. It was over eight inches, close to nine, and was it thick! And oh, was it heaven to have a cock in my mouth again, after so long! Mouths and cocks were made for each other. The feel of skin of the glans and the corona is one of the great sensual pleasures of the tongue. As I moved my wet lips and tongue up and down, I could feel the pulses of firmness coming, in response. He was ready. But I decided to give his balls some tonguing. He shivered and moaned as I zapped my tongue back and forth over one ball and then the other. His fingers began to dig into my shoulders, as his tension rose. So, I began to explore his anus with my fucking finger to see how much he could take. I put that pecker back in my hot juicy mouth to keep it pleased, while I went exploring with my finger. And when I pushed it in, he gave out a gasp and squeezed. I looked and his head was turned up with an expression of anguished ecstasy or ecstatic agony, I don't know which. He enjoyed the finger fuck! I sucked some more to bring that big dick back to perfect rigidity...down as far as I could go before the gagging would start, then slowly back up with the tongue wonking away, up over that magnificent rim, then back down again.

When he was ready, the pulsing of firmness over and the glans so hard it was going to burst, I went back to his balls for some more tonguing and I give him not one, but two, more fingers up his asshole. That bastard just gave out the deepest, emptiest groan you can imagine. I pulled down my pants and sat down on the floor with my cock sticking up. The Nivea cream was in my swimming bag beside me, so I put some on my cock. I said to the guy, "Sit on it!"

He stepped out of his pants and lowered himself onto my stuff with his thighs bulging and his torso muscles quivering. And, oh god, did that hot sweet ass feel good! This guy obviously had had practice. With his beautiful thighs working like hydraulic lifts, he raised and lowered and raised and lowered his ass with perfect rhythm. And now, I was ready. I got that big tip back in my mouth and I worked the shaft with my hand, and I could feel the pulsing and that tip got so hard and tight and then, squirt!...squirt!...squirt!...squirt! I thought it would never end. It filled my mouth. It started pouring out of my mouth, into my hand, into my beard, and still squirt!...squirt!...squirt! All the while, his torso muscles rippling away, his head thrown back in pure pleasure and that ass of his never stopped its slow rhythmic up and down stroke. It was too much. Now, it was my turn and I gave him all I had. Right up that beautifully sculptured ass. Right there on the floor of my office.

When he saw I had come, he just laid himself on me and I could embrace him for the first time. I felt those hard shoulders and back with the pronounced spinal indentation, those firm buttocks. I was in heaven! After a while, I noticed he was falling asleep, so I nuzzled his ear and bit his earlobe. He gave a start. I whispered to him the best cliché I could think of…

"You've never told me your name."

He didn't laugh. He just matter-of-factly said, "Lynn".

I said, "Lynn, that class you just signed up for?"

"Yes?"

"Well, it's supposed to meet right now."

"Oh?"

"So, we have to put our clothes back on."

"We do?" He still wanted to go back to sleep.

"Yes!"

"Oh!" He got up and put on what little clothes he had on. "Here, let me stuff that back in for you," I said.

The poor guy. Even after his hard-on had gone, it was still too long for those cut-offs. We tried packing it in another way: straight up. But then, he started to get hard again and started rubbing himself against me, dreamily. Obviously, this guy was a pleasure machine! Finally, I managed to tuck it all in. I wound it around his hip and tucked the end up his ass.

We went off to class, together. But when I tried to lecture, I wasn't too successful. Whenever I went to stroke my beard, I would find this gooey mess that startled me. Lynn didn't learn much that day, either. He fell asleep. And then, there was this cute little blonde trick who kept fondling himself, as he eyed Lynn's basket. I guess he saw me watching him. So, he came up after class and said that he needed some advice about his program. So, what could I do? I invited him, etc.

Jim

Letter #3 – November 16, 1978

Dearest Lynn,

Sweetheart, here I am again! Not where I want so much to be...in your arms. I am in bed, the kids are asleep, and Sally has gone off to New Orleans for six whole days! I have an empty place beside me. Oh, how I wish you could be here! I miss you terribly. I think of you every day. I think that my six months with you were the most serenely happy time of my life I never felt so <u>natural</u> as when we were together. The only thing wrong was that we couldn't let our love for each other take its natural course and grow and grow and grow. But it has, anyway. I still love you very much.

I enjoyed your jack off letter and your picture (-handsome dog, you). I think I can find something to send you. Did he really bring back a Latin bus boy? You know I got hard as soon as I read that. But I don't think we should spend all our time writing jack off letters to one another. (By the way, I do have my cock in my hand, with Nivea cream. It's next best to having you sucking away.) We have so much to catch up on. I never wrote you about Bryce Canyon. You haven't told me about EST. I do want to know all about it. I would like to know something about how San Francisco and Berkley voted on the Briggs Amendment. I know the state turned it down by 55% or so. That was so refreshing to learn. And we, in turn, did not pass our version of Jarvis Gann, although a mild tax limitation did pass.

The most interesting thing that I have done since I wrote you last was...you realized, of course, that the black stud of my last letter was not real. Or, rather, he is real; he was packing a marvelous basket and I did give it a relishing look. But I never propositioned him. HOWEVER. Writing that letter did something to me. Remember, I mentioned that I had my eye on a little Asian who came to the pool? Shortly after I sent off

that letter to you, I found myself alone in the shower with him.
He started vigorously soaping up his crotch, while looking at
me. So, I started soaping my shaft while watching him. His
eyes lit up. So, I propositioned him then and there. I ended
up paying $15 for a motel room! But it was worth it. I had
never propositioned anyone at Pentwater (my school), before.
He's from Thailand and will be returning after the school term.
He's going for an MA in Economics. I'd say he was 25ish. Then,
the following week, I asked him again but he had a class. So,
as I was walking out of the pool, I noticed a curly headed
Italian, blow drying his hair and eyeing the meat as it passed.
I chalked him up as gay. Later, it turned out his locker was
near mine and he was drying himself. I saw that he was hung.
So, I looked; ordinarily, I am furtive. But this time, I said
what the hell, no one was around. He saw me looking and dried
the dear crotch, that long thing, again...ever so carefully.
So, I smiled and said, "That's mighty nice." He smiled back and
the dear thing grew some. So, I just said as nonchalantly as I
could, "Any time you want it sucked, just let me know." HONEST.
He hesitated. Then, he asked, "Where did you have in mind, the
john?" "No," I said, "My house." It was a day I could use it.
So, his thing got even longer. It's amazing that no one came
by. By the time he got his underpants on, it was hard. He was
a little like you: heavy five o'clock beard and was currently
singing in the musical, "Irene". But he was a willowier build.
Both he and the Thor had to come twice.

The next week, there was my Italian friend, again. This
time, he invited me to his apartment. But also, he is gone.
He's transferring to another college and has left.

Then, the next week, there was my trip to Lansing,
Michigan, state capital. The fellow I stayed over with,
however, has turned into a strange, timid soul since he got his

divorce. He's not especially attractive, either (bald with silly toupee). I found him something of a chore. I probably will not sleep with him, again.

So, as you can see, I have had four good homosexual experiences, since I wrote last. But none with people I will see, again. This week, I got a real shock. One of my students, a beautiful blue-eyed blonde guy, was at a locker near mine, when I got out of the pool. It was pool closing time but he was going to use the steam room which always has one or two, sometimes more, gays in it. One with an earring and a butterfly tattooed on his ass. He stripped right by me, as we talked. He didn't wear underpants and his cock was easily seven inches just hanging there. My heart leapt into my mouth. His body was marvelous. But I had no real clue that he might be gay. So, I just did nothing. As I was leaving, however, he came out of the steam room and started talking to an older guy who I've had my eyes on; I'm reasonably sure he is gay. I could see this guy was semihard as he talked to my student. Their conversation was low and I got the distinct feeling this guy had had him before.

I was in a tizzy! I even developed a face twitch. I had to masturbate twice just so I could get him off my mind. And that is where it stands now. He was in class today with a beautiful smile. But he is on great kidding relations with two girls. So, I suppose he is bi. I don't know what to do. I hate having chicken fever! I want to be with you so that I can be normal, again!

By the way, I prefer your cock to all the ones I've had. I think a thick, round nob with a flaring corona (or whatever it's called) is much more sensuous and exciting than these little buds sitting on top of nine-inch stems. And the thick nob, sweetheart, is what you have. I can feel it still in my mouth (and my ass...oh!)

And that's all about my sex life. I hope you are not
denying yourself. Did you ever have a return engagement with
the EST fellow with the poor timing? How much of your jack off
letter is based on fact? (Anything can happen in Berkley, so
don't think I'm silly to ask.)

My friend, Doug Jones, was in Michigan just about two hours
away, visiting his mother for a week. But we never met. He
called but the night he was to be in town, we had invitations to
dinner. I asked how he was; he sounded cheerful when he said,
"Fine!" So, maybe he has had treatments for his cancer and been
cured. I didn't want to ask, explicitly. Let me know if you
ever contact him.

And let me know how your activities with the church
revitalization committee goes, and how Vickie's weight goes, and
how the gang is. Give my regards to them all.

And now as for Bryce...it was a complete surprise. Coming
from the west, you see so much red stone that by the time we
reached Bryce, I thought it would be too much. But it was
entirely unlike anything else; I called it Munchkinland.
Something about it...unreal. Tall spires that seem to be made
of brightly cobbled stucco: reds, pinks, and whites in layers.
They extend in rows for miles. Fantastic! - like something you
would say could only have been concocted in a Walt Disney movie
(or MGM, if they did Oz). You can view them from above, a
panoramic view, a la Grand Canyon, and you can hike down among
them, which is also amazing. The peculiar spires are the result
of the fact that the rock is quite young and so, still soft.
The erosion process makes it look like dried mud, which is
probably what it was, once.

The Grand Canyon, Zion, and Bryce form a sequence of rocks
from the oldest; I think hundreds of millions of years. Even
one billion, I think, at the base of the Grand Canyon to a

couple of hundred thousand in Bryce. I'm not going to take the trouble to check the dates. But southern Utah must be a geologist's paradise.

For Christmas, we are driving to Florida to visit my folks. We will leave on December 15th and get back January 5th, or so. I will renew my tan. I have acquired back all the pounds I lost on our camping trip. So, I'm about where I was when you last saw me. Next summer, Sally has a teaching position for six weeks near Boulder, Colorado. So, that's as close as I'll get to you. I may even get to Denver in May (convention). Alas, not very close, is it? The Pacific coast convention for 1979 is scheduled for San Diego. I will submit a paper to read but the competition is tough. If I get a paper accepted, I can probably get my school to pay my costs. That's the only way I could afford it. That jewel tree has really set us back. Then, on top of that, I gave Sally an emerald set in white gold with three diamonds, for her fortieth birthday. You need something to get through your fortieth. But the end result is that I have literally one dollar in the savings account and I am going to have to take out a loan to pay my winter taxes.

Recently, my income tax returns were audited. I took my box with receipts to the office and so impressed the guy (or confounded him, I don't know which) that they accepted my return as filed! It's like losing one's virginity. I've been audited and I got away scot free! (Now, I wonder if I've been overpaying!)

As for my day to day life, it is teaching and coming home to write, write, write. I'm still working on that goddam free-will paper, or rather, papers. I seem to be embarked on a Laura Ingalls-Wilder reading marathon with the kids, and getting set for winter.

All the leaves have dropped, except for the dead leaves
that cling to the oaks. Frosts are a nightly occurrence. Soon,
there will be snow and the midday temperature, which now hovers
around 50, will go to 40, then 30. In January and February, it
will be 20. Those are the days of the winter drearies. Clouds
will obscure the sun for weeks on end. I once counted five
weeks without ever seeing the sun, except for a two hours period
on one day. But that's still a month away.

And now to dream about sleeping with you and coming.

Love,

Jim

The Cares o' Love

He

The cares o' Love are sweeter far
    Than onie other pleasure;
And if sae Dear its sorrows are,
    Enjoyment, what a treasure!

She

I fear to try, I dare na try
    A passion sae ensnaring;
For light's her heart and blithe's her song
    That for nae man is caring.

~ Robert Burns (1759-1796)

Letter #4 - December 1, 1978

Three letters in a row! It's fun just to "listen" to you from your bed as you just chat. I will call. I've been kicking myself for not doing it on that free week I had when I wrote you last. It has occurred to me several times. And I always knew, in a sense, you wanted me to, since you put your number on the address slip, which I have. But...I don't know why I haven't. I always found a reason. But I think if we don't have to say something IMPORTANT to justify LONG DISTANCE, it will be easier. We can talk about the view out your window, your luscious lips. The other thing is you say, "Soon." But you are, for example, in Carmel, today(?). I will be off for Florida the day after tomorrow and won't be back until January 3rd. So, it will have to be this January.

One thing about your letter bothered me. Don't let your love for me tie your hands. Here is a luscious green-eyed thing mooning at you and you say you'll have to tell him about us! Dearest, remember that night you almost threw me out of your apartment and your life? Think back and try to recover that frame of mind. You were absolutely sensible, then. I am wondering if you still are, if you are going to let our letter affair interfere with your finding a complete and fulfilling relationship. My love for you can only be fulfilled by my seeing you completely happy with another man. That's the way it has to be.

Enough of that. I am glad to see you keeping your hand in things...fist, no less! I haven't been opened up at all. However, I came out to an eight-incher, at least, in the showers, today. But because of scheduling problems, it will have to wait until January.

Remember the guy I had in class who sent me into chicken fever? Well, first I got a cold, so I left off swimming for two weeks. I even missed two classes. So, it subsided. But when I came back, he would wait for me as class left, to chat. And the fever came back. I really felt he was after me. So, yesterday there he was at the pool. So, I cruised him gently with my eyes, asked how he acquired his physique, etc. I could tell he was on the alert for a proposition. He delayed dressing. So, I asked him what he wanted me to ask. I said, "Wait and I'll walk back with you." When we were half way, I said I was going to eat and asked would he want to join me. Yes, again. But I had no indication, really. So, when he started asking me if I was married, I said no. He pressed for my reason. So, I said I was gay. You know, I bet if I told him how he had set everything up and had been for over two weeks, he wouldn't believe it. Then, he told me he had gay feelings and accepted them but did not act on them. THE BASTARD.

Then, I told him I lied. Actually, I was married and had two kids. He said, "So! I've just been shafted." After he squirmed a little, I assured him that our exchange of confidences was accurate, that I was gay. I also assured him that I would not proposition him; oh, the pain. He was relieved at that. And so, we chatted about gayness, etc., and Sally got a good session, last night. I saw him again today and he talked a little more. He's into a girl, right now. But I swear he's going to come over. He is fascinated with the gay scene. He hung around again, today, watching the steam room. Once he saw me go in half hard and the eight-incher played a little in the showers (I say eight-incher because that is all there is to him: short, dumpy, sort of effeminate), I can see him go gulp with the forbidden fruit attracting him. Perhaps when he decides to go, he'll land in my arms. Twenty years old. Does gymnastics and swimming. Big steel blue eyes. I can tell my sperm

producer has been hyperactive. I have a pleasure glow
throughout my abdomen. But oh, the pain, too.

Generally speaking, the scene here is dismal. Forty-two
guys were arrested a month ago at a rest stop on a highway in
the course of one week of TV surveillance of the toilet! One
night that hits the papers. The next night, there is a story
about two teachers in a high school being reinstated until
charges are tried. The paper doesn't say the two stories are
connected. The next night, there's a story about parents
picketing the school about the reinstatement; and-so-it-goes
story.

The subject of the gays in San Francisco came up at a
dinner party, Friday…

Got interrupted, sweetheart. I've been sitting here
grading papers and, as usual, my thoughts drifted to you. I've
taken your picture out of the drawer and given it a long kiss.
Now, my cock is crunching up in my tight pants. I love you so
much. And I know you'll understand and forgive my chicken
fever! You should be here, or I should be there to get your
antidote, the peace and security of your mature love.

So, I was saying how I attended a dinner party and San
Francisco gayety. I just cut all questions short when I was
asked how I could take a one-third gay population. I said,
"Where a guy plugs his cock is about as important to me as where
he parks his car." The host looked at the hostess and asked,
"Has Kathy (their daughter) gone upstairs?" I look at the
hostess. She is beet red. Another guy says, "Yeah, but what
about where they drop their soap?" I try to lighten the mood by
saying, "Well now, if it were my driveway...". The discussion
concludes with the host saying, "Well, I wouldn't want to live
there!" The host and hostess, incidentally, are authors of a

book on sexuality in Victorian literature. You wouldn't suspect they would be prudes.

My gay hairdresser, by the way, is fun to talk to. The only one in Michigan I could go to on the day of the Pentwater – Pentwater State football game and never have the subject come up. What did we talk about? Why, Betty Ford's facial, of course! It turns out "Jonathan" (really John) has had $2,000 worth of work done on his own face. So, for all I know, he may be sixty. His hair is a different color every time I go in. Next time, he says, I'll see him without a beard. -Knock-knock-

3:30...grading done, Christmas party done, three sheets to the wind done, and I'm going to have to cut this short, darling. (I get a thrill just calling you "darling".) Merry, Merry Xmas and a Gay New Year. As for the present, hold off if you haven't already sent it, since I prefer it not hanging around the mail box for weeks. Do you remember that little book of sayings you gave me, once? I have it by my desk at home. I look at it, occasionally. They sound just like you! I have a novel by Patricia Nell Warren I've been meaning to send off to you. This one about a priest and an Indian; my two favorite childhood fantasies combined into one. But it doesn't have the suspense of *The Front Runner*.

Now, I must run before the bank closes. XX Love XX
Jim

Letter #5 – January 18, 1979

Dear Heart,

Evan went right to work on the Denver trip, after our telephone conversation. The very next morning, I walked into the office and my chairman said, "So, you want to go to Denver. I've got some money." There are still some problems. There's not enough for everyone. But I and one other fellow have the inside track on it, because we at least submitted papers which, however, were rejected.

You asked how my writing was going. Well, I write, and write, and write. But nothing published in the last two years; only seven rejection notices. I feel rejected. I have one out now to a journal called *The Philosophical Review*. They say they reject 96% of the articles submitted to them. So, I expect rejection number eight within a month. Perhaps Evan could help out, there. It would be helping you (I know he's your guardian angel, not mine). If I got a paper accepted by that journal, I would probably get a $500 bonus next year and that would finance some more get-togethers for us.

I cannot say exactly what the date in Denver is. Nobody here knows! (That's why I've delayed writing.) I think I am going to have to call the national office to find out. But the weekend that seems most likely is April 20th to 22nd, the weekend after Easter. The second most likely is the previous weekend, Easter, but I doubt that.

Do you think we can make up for nine months lost time in three days?? Well, we can certainly try.

And I am so, so, so sorry you have orgied yourself right into bed with a nasty cold. Partying with guys who dance with their cocks out. Feeling each other up in the hot tub. You live such a quiet life.

As you can see, I'm envious. No sex (worth mentioning) for almost three months. You, my darling, are going to have the skin worn right off your lips and your cock, not to mention sore ear lobes, sore tits, very, very sensitive balls, and an ass that won't remember how to close up. And I certainly hope I have the same!

Have to stop here to go to lecture. But you should know how happy it made me to hear how completely at peace you are with yourself. And I am so glad you discovered Evan! Really! I have trouble with God. As a philosopher, I think of God as the Creator Almighty. That is just too awesome, too overpowering, and too remote. But a faith and trust in Evan is close to the notion of the Holy Spirit that dwells within us. I admire you for the faith you have. That is what brought us together in the first place. Although we didn't talk that much about it, it always remained one of the things that attracted me to you and still does.

I think about you, always. In my imagination, I am always talking with you. Last night...well, I have started taking bridge lessons. And I sat down with the three older women. One asked us about getting together extra nights for practice. When she called the house to set up a night, Sally wanted to know what it was about. I said that I was arranging for my night out with the girls. And in my mind, I turned to you and said, "Wasn't that a campy remark?" And I imagined your hearty guffaws. I remember very well. I love you, sweetheart. Can't wait to get back to making you come and hugging you as you fall on me. Yum yum.

Love,

Jim

Letter #6 - January 27, 1979

Dear Sweetheart,

Don't bother Evan about my paper. There's nothing he can do. I just got another rejection, dated January 17. Not even an angel can change the past.

Not even "Superman", even if the movie shows him changing the past. I don't recommend "Superman" to Bay Area people, even if looking at Superman is one of the nicest turn-ons I can imagine. Absolutely gorgeous! But they play down his basket.

(Resumed writing in the PM.) After class, after swim...eyes tearing from all the chlorine. Back to Superman's basket...oh, yes, the reason I don't recommend the movie is that (you can tell all the interruptions from my pen color changes) it contains every Bay Area person's nightmare. Being on the Golden Gate Bridge as the big quake hits. I know every time I went over the bridge, the twinge of fear hit. But it is otherwise a fun flick. I enjoyed the double entendre, as Clark Kent looks into one of our new-fangled telephone booths affording no privacy and has to improvise in a revolving door!

And as I say, he is gorgeous. Which reminds me of you. By now, your cold is better and you are back into things. By the way, the dyslexic fist fuckee, speaking of into things, are you still into him (at least for kicks, or is it fists)?

You said you now believe Kit knows that, to speak of another gorgeous hunk just like his father, knows that you are gay. Did you confirm that with Eugenie, or are you just picking up the vibes? I know that if I were in your shoes, I would be really torn between letting it go as unspoken mutual knowledge or making it explicit. The deciding consideration for me would be, "Which would protect and preserve a loving relationship with your sons, better?" Your instincts are your best guide. It would be so much easier if Kit were gay! Imagine what a wholesome and natural entry into the gay world a guy would have if he knew his dad was gay, too! No family hassles, no isolation, hiding closety feelings, etc. And with his looks, he would have the pick of the crop. Maybe he is (more wishful thinking).

And you must let me know about *The Advocate* experience. That sounds like just the sort of thing I could use. Maybe you can let me have it, vicariously.

Snow: it's getting me down. Yesterday, I got my car stuck in the driveway. Finally, I jacked it up and pushed the car over. Then, I sit down and notice drip, drip, drip. So, I shovel a balcony where the snow had drifted up to the windows. Back to road. But still drip, drip, drip. The leak must be coming down the wall from the roof. So, I go up and salt the ice buildup on the roof. Then, the water softener...it's constantly recharging. Which reminds me, I have to go to the hardware store to buy a nut for the toilet bowl seat because the old one rusted out. I hate WORLDLY THINGS! Cars! Houses! Snow! Water softeners! Toilet bowls! More snow is forecast for tonight. It's now above my knees. Fortunately, the temperature has gone up to its usual 20 degrees. A week ago, it was averaging -5 and I would have to set a certain faucet dripping to keep that pipe from freezing. I would have to finagle a fuse with the battery cables to start my car.

SHIIIIIIIT!

And now, this shitty manuscript rejection. I'm in a lousy mood. You are my sunshine, my only sunshine. You make me happy, when skies are gray. If you only hold me...am I quoting?? It is true, nevertheless. Your happiness is my sunshine.

And it just brightened up, outside. No, the sun did not come out; it just brightened up. Even that is worth something.

And now, off I go to a goddam meeting. Sweetheart, I can't wait to be with you, again. It's all I can look forward to.

Love and kisses,

Jim

Wednesday, 31st...another four inches, last night. Shoveled the drive, late to school, noticed leak in another place. Arrrgh!

Letter #7 – February 14, 1979

Dearest,

Happy St. Valentine's Day, my love. You will receive it late but today is Valentine's Day. Kisses to your lips, your eyes, your nipples, your neck, etc., etc., etc.

I have got to get into the habit of stealing time here and there to add to a letter. I usually wait for a big block of time to come up. And when is that? Never. The last two weeks have been hectic. I had two speeches to deliver, exams to grade, Alice had chicken pox, the garage door wouldn't work...

And you, sweetheart...five letters! I think if my secretary ever asks, I will have only one credible explanation. "Just a girl in Berkley who's crazy about me, wants me to leave my wife and live with her. Name's Lynn. Oh, you knew that? Actually, it's quite platonic. After all, what can you really do over 2,000 miles? My cock isn't quite that long." On second thought, I think I'll delete that last part.

First, I want to tell you how I reacted to your letter about telling Kit. I opened it while walking to the library. And as so often happens when I read your letters, I started getting hard. So, I was giving a test that day and I put the letters away to read them when I could cross my legs. So, I opened your letter in class. I did it! I did it! And as I read, my heart began to pound and my hands trembled. I have lived with this problem of yours for a year, too! I didn't stop trembling for a long time. All my own fears were reawakened. I remembered how close I came to telling Sally when she arrived in San Francisco, and how I became important for five weeks with everybody. So, your telling Kit was *traumatic for me*! Then, I got that very same day, your letter about how good it is to come clean by coming out, and you said you hoped that the message was coming at the right time. Well, sweetheart, it came at the wrong time. I was still trembling!

However, I am now no longer trembling. I'm very happy for you, not only that you have that off shoulders but also, that you are fortunate enough to have such mature children. Kit must be a remarkable personality...what is he, 17? But now that the ice is broken, you might be able to get an honest picture of what caused his school difficulties a year and a half ago, I think it was. I remember thinking at the time that it may have been the result of his discovering that you were gay and not knowing how to fit that in with his own values and feelings. However, maybe it's better not to put Kit into a position where he would have to confess to negative feelings about you. He has made a remarkable adjustment. You are one of the lucky ones, admit it. For you, coming out has not led to any alienation of your family, divorce excepted, but your children and brother accept it. For many, it's not so lucky.

One of your recommendations to me is something I think would be good for me: write a letter "to" Sally, coming out to her. I dread it and probably will put it off until I have a really big chunk of time, like when I retire or something. But actually, I think it would be a useful exercise.

I do daydream about how to be free to marry you, so to speak. Even if I kept my job here, that would leave May through August to be with you as well as some weeks or weekends during the thirty-six weeks of the term.

Thank you for the Christmas present of the call. I will call again but perhaps it won't be until the beginning of March; Sally will be in Dallas for the weekend. As for the trip to Denver, don't you think twice about the cost. It will only cost $156 and change if you include a Saturday night in your stay in Denver. I still don't have firm dates, yet. But when I do, you can buy tickets and I will send you a check (bank check, of course) for the actual cost. If Sally can buy jewel trees, I can spend a mere 7% of that amount to fly in my favorite call boy from San Fran, can't I? Now, I will go back to correcting homework, awhile. Soon, I'll be daydreaming about you again, and I'll return to this letter.

John break. Emma's home. You asked how I'm doing with Laura Ingalls-Wilder. Well, Emma has been reading them on her own, now. She's reading *Winter Days*, right now. She's also read most of the *Mrs. Piggle Wiggle* books and *Charlotte's Web*. She just turned eight. I know I wasn't doing that much reading at her age. I was compiling a word book. I had collected 600 words, before my parents told me there were such things as dictionaries. Not only the words, but their meanings, too! The story of my life. Someone always beats me to it. When I read now, I prefer the *Paddington* series; they are witty. *The Little House in the Woods* has an ending that really got me all choked up. I, too, have a sentimental streak.

It is now Thursday morning. How I wish to sleep with you, wake up to the touch of your hairy body, and squirm all over you. We should try to have three nights together. Oh god, is my cock hard! I want you to know that I enjoy your cutouts. The one about *Arthur* having a genius for avoiding the hackneyed phrase is going up in my office. But your others are obviously cut from *The Advocate*. All I have to do is turn them over and see snippets of those gorgeous bodies. Do you know what that does to a sex-starved guy like me? If you are reading *The Advocate* regularly, watch for Denver ads. I would like to see if there's at least a gay restaurant. But a gay motel with gay porn on the TV would be IDEAL! I have a *Damron* guide. But aside from the gay movies, it looks like teeny bopper bars, only. Anyway, I hope if you are now branching out in your reading to picture books, like *Blue Boy*, *Colt*, *Playgirl*, *After Dark*, etc., I hope you bring them along.

Anyway, cock back down. I am really distressed to hear about your symptoms. I didn't think they would be VD. I never heard of dizziness as a symptom. It certainly is something to be concerned over. I hope it turns out to be nothing much; perhaps it is only those swoonings associated with love sickness. Let me know what the doctor says...and try putting some beans in your salad.

Thursday evening. Maybe writing to you will put me back into a good mood. The furnace is on the blink again, one week after a guy sold us a $95 switch. Evidently, nothing was wrong with our switch because it's the same problem. And my air conditioner in the car is on the fritz. That means no defogger or deicer. And I didn't mention my cracked filling, which has now led to "root canal" work on one tooth. At least the garage door is now fixed. Fuck worldly things! I do enjoy the cartoons you send me. I remember the *Arthur* with all the hair. Does the *New Yorker* have an *Arthur* series or something?

One thing nice...there are now two excellent bread bakers in town. (Not brioche, yet, but someday.) The French bread from one of them is the most aromatically delicious bread I've ever smelled.

Another nice thing...the little Thai guy did not return to Thailand, after all. He's started coming to the baths; i.e., school saunas, again. I invited him to lunch. He refused but later showed up at my table. Perhaps someday we'll get it on together. He seemed interested, then, but when I asked him yesterday, he said he couldn't. Perhaps he really couldn't, who knows? I still see the one I had a crush on in December but that has cooled. He has been keeping his distance a bit. Quite a change from the way he behaved in December. Fickle youth.

I've tried to figure out the name of my guardian angel. No
luck. I come up with Adrian. But that's the name of the most
beautiful guy in my high school class. (But he wasn't the one I
was sick with love for; his name was Rob.)

Friday morning...one meeting down, one to go. Car in for
fixing. I'm down in the union office. And just had the
satisfaction of uncovering a gross error in some administrative
documents. The guy (whose name is Jack Butler – you can imagine
what we do to that) can't read an annual report and so, gave the
impression that the university is socking away millions each
year.

I'd much rather go to an EST meeting, preferably with you.
The one in Detroit is impossible for me, as you probably
guessed. Actually, I have a pretty upbeat view of life when I'm
with you. You "est" me really well, especially with Nivea
cream. (How many cases do you think we'll need?)

You've written me so many times, I can't remember all the
things I should respond to! Miscellaneous item: I don't really
expect Bernardo to write. And go right ahead and be jealous. I
love it. I didn't forget our anniversary and was going to send
you a card. But I just couldn't find one appropriate to gay
lovers. I was also going to send you a schmaltzy big
sentimental Valentine heart with ribbons and bows and gushy
verse. But I let that slip past. Same with Chinese New Year,
Ground Hog Day (a big event, here). Now, I'll probably miss St.
Patty's Day. Incidentally, I was relieved not to get a big
Valentine card in my box. That would have sent my secretary off
snickering.

So, remember, my big, darling, handsome man...I love you, I
love you, I love you. And in two months, I will have three days
of ecstasy in your arms. And do get better. Find out what that

dizziness is. It sounded like you have had this symptom before,
although I can't remember you mentioning it, before.

I have been meaning to give you my brother, Jerry's,
address and he yours, so that if I should die or something, we
could spare Sally the burden of a post mortem discovery of
letters, etc. What a morbid way to end a letter. I'm sorry.
I'll make up for it by composing a jack off letter for you.

Love and more love,

Jim

Letter #8 – March 3, 1979

Saturday

Hello, dearest.

I'm taking a break from my annual duel of wits with the IRS.
I'm pretty good at it. Last year, I deducted $4200 in
sabbatical living expenses (among other things), was audited two
months or more ago and got it all accepted as filed. This year,
I have so many paper receipts, I'm going daffy. I just totaled
$800 in supermarket receipts. This translates into $100 more in
my tax refund. A good day's work.

You see, I DO take responsibility for my life. Because I
do, all those miserable things I complained about are fixed: the
leak; the garage door motor; the transmitter; my cracked
filling; the car defroster; the water softener; the oven heating
unit...

Oh! I just saw a V-shaped flock of Canadian geese flying
south out my window! One more sign. The thaw has been in
progress for over a week. It is raining, right now. The snow
still covers our roof and the ground all around. But it is down
from its several feet to about six to nine inches, now. The
painfully slow revival of life has started. Perhaps in two
weeks, all snow will be gone. (We had 80 inches, this year.)
Then, the lakes will thaw and then the smell of unfrozen earth
will hit me. The way I gauge the melting is by watching the
exposure of sumac canes. The rabbits eat the bark off them. As
the snow melts, the uneaten bark is exposed. Soon, I will take
responsibility for the apple-cedar rust that weakens my
beautiful hawthorn thicket. That involves weeks of picking
little balls off the cedars. Cedar balls don't do much for me.

I suppose you'll say I'm taking responsibility for the
wrong things; that they are a substitute. You're right. I know
you and Evan have decided what's right for me; maybe Anderson is

in on it, too. BUT. I'm pretty sure it will be a while before
you find my suitcase in hand at your door. These are steps I
simply am not prepared to take.

Three things tie me down: causing pain to Sally and the
children; the embarrassment of coming out; the comfort and
security of my present arrangements. I have known my reasons
since the Summer of '77. I don't know which motives are the
strongest; they vary from moment to moment. Last year, there
was another reason: I realized breaking with Sally in a strange
place would have meant for Sally a total washout of her
sabbatical and a compounding of insecurity in her and the
children. I do love you and you would think that would be
enough to push me over. But I am such a fatalist...see, you
were right about responsibility...I feel I have established the
course of my life and now must live it out. Isn't that also
being responsible?

Oh, well.

I am including an excerpt of a book by Edward Wilson, *On
Human Nature*. It is the nicest argument in our favor that I
have seen. According to Wilson's theory, for the hundreds of
thousands of years while humans were just hunters and gatherers
of food, we homosexuals were so useful to our families that even
though we had few children, our heterosexual families prospered
and had more kids. And that is how the genetic basis for
homosexuality has been passed on from generation to generation.
For some of those genes are carried by our heterosexual
relatives. You may know of Edward Wilson, the sociobiology
controversy. But even if it is controversial, I wouldn't be at
all surprised if it were true. We are good for society!
Besides being more intelligent, more people-oriented, especially
man-oriented, more with it, more more-more, more outgoing and

cumming. (I guess this is sexist; mustn't forget our lesbian
brothers.)

You won't like what Edward Wilson says about EST, though.
Is it true that they won't let you get out of your chair to go
to the bathroom? Wilson says that!

And now, while I think of it, here is my brother's address.
I will write to him, giving him yours. He, incidentally, is
101% opposed to my breaking up with Sally. He thinks my talk
about love is thoroughly childish. However, his hard exterior
is partly defensive. He and his lover of five years are slowly
but surely drifting apart. His lover, Brax, is bi and the girl
now lives with them! Well, after he gave me a stern lecture
about love, I just told him that I didn't think love was silly;
for example, I loved him and that wasn't silly. That shut him
up. I haven't told him I loved him in thirty years! (Isn't it
sweet how Jimmy loves Billy?)

I can't believe your church! Around here, they just
arrested three bookstore owners for showing pictures like that
(e.g., *Hustler* mag). No kidding. The john at the library is
kept locked to prevent...no kidding again, it was in the
newspaper...to prevent, oh horror, homosexual activity. Last
Fall, forty-two men were seen on a hidden TV camera, engaging
in, oh horrors, homosexual activity in a stall at an interstate
rest stop. And two were high school teachers. It wasn't clear
from the reports whether they were together. But what is clear
is that they were hounded out of their jobs.

You not only have a wonderful family; you live in a
wonderful society. But the fact that Eugenie was the only one
who had to raise her hand that two gays were a turn-on shows
that it is still hypocritical, to some extent. What kind of
picture was it? I would really like to know. Nude and kissing?

Or, 69 or sodomy? Everyone should have been turned on by two men LOVING one another.

Guess I'll get back to work.

Supper's over. This was the weekend I was going to call you. But Sally decided at the last minute not to go to Dallas. I will call soon, though. This, by the way, starts a week vacation for me. How nice it would be to fly to you for the week.

I'm glad to see that you are fully recovered. However, don't bet it was all in your mind! Think, instead, how little we understand of the physical world around us. All you can conclude is that the doctor <u>didn't know</u> what ailed you. Don't convert his ignorance of the physical into knowledge of the mental. I wouldn't be surprised if you were suffering from an unknown viral infection from which you recovered, in due course. The moral, of course, is that the next time it happens, if it does, hit the sack just as you did, reach under the mattress and start plugging away; now get some rest. Anyway, I'm glad your mind is at ease, now.

Wednesday

Dear Sweetheart. I just got your letter about the untying of the apron strings and I feel for you. Now is the time I should be with you and comfort you in my arms. If only I could be yours, I would try to fill the vacuum in your life. I was going to say, "fill the hole", but I don't mean to be cracking jokes, or cheeks; oh, well, here we go. I should tell you it was almost unbearable, this morning. I didn't jack off but I should have. No sooner had I awoke, I started fantasizing I was with you. I imagined sleepily turning over and finding your warm body beside me, asleep. I nuzzled up to you, caressing you with my arms and lips, hands on your nipples. From toe to head, I was intermingled with you. But you just slept on. I moved my

fingers slowly down your body to your pubic hairs and played
with them. Then, I lovingly and lightly stroked your hard cock.
My, but it must be a nice dream you're having. I decide to make
it nicer and work my way under the covers to your mouth-filling,
yummy cock, which I remember so fondly. There I am, in a hot
tent of covers, all alone with your pulsating penis! It still
smells of Nivea cream from last night, some dried cum on it. I
lick it clean. Then, in it goes. Down go my lips, my tongue
working all around back up, then down, up...oh, so slowly...then
down firmly.

I just got mine out of my pants. I've just got to cum.
Just a few days ago, I was thinking I had lost interest in sex.
But it's just the lack of proper stimulation.

You move, slightly. Are you awake? I can't tell. Your
cock is; that's for sure. I slip a finger in your ass, as I
suck away. You grunt. I massage your prostate, gently. All
alone in my tent; me, your cock with its wonderful glans, your
sensitive balls, which I will attack any minute now, and your
prostate. All mine.

Then, you grunt and roll over! Oh, dastardly fate! But
now, your ass stares me in the face. You are the only person I
would rim. But it's not the right position. It is only good
for one thing. So, I squirm up along your body until my cock
feels its comfy cozy. My head is now by yours. You have a
smile on your face. Are you asleep? As I pump back and forth,
slowly (just as I'm doing, now), I look at your beautiful face.
I feel your beautiful dark hair against my cheek. Oh, the
pleasure and the desire! Pure love pours out of me into you;
first, spiritually...soul to soul. Then, physically with the
excruciating ecstasy, as you turn your lips to mine. I CUM!
Ahhhhh.

Mmmmmm, that was good. It's not easy, you know, to write with one hand and jack off with the other, while kneeling before the toilet in a locked bathroom, while your wife types away and your sick kid reads, *Pippi Longstocking*, on the other side of the wall. But even so, it was good.

I should tell you that I emulate you as a father. Your open lovingness with your children has been important to me. If you thought I was a disciplinarian last year, you should have seen me a year or two before, when I was so wound up in unionizing. I would demand my way much the same way as the tyrant administrator I was fighting. He, incidentally, has finally, at long last, found someone who would hire him, three years after he was told he would have to leave, two years after he was relieved of his post as Academic Vice President. He is to become Chancellor of the Little Hilo branch of the University of Hawaii. I, too, am much more loving with my children and I give them more of my time. I see now again from your experience that we must enjoy them, while we have them. They grow up and away so fast.

Love,

Jim

Letter #9 – March 8, 1979

Dearest Love,

I am so excited. I can't wait until we meet in Denver. I may just throw my arms around you in the airport and give you a torrid, sensual French kiss. What will I have to lose, standing there in my flowery bathing suit?

Anyway, after I had sealed your letter, I learned for sure that the dates are April 19 to 21. We will be at the Denver Hilton, unless we can find something better. I have gotten your check, which is enclosed. Furthermore, I start my vacation then, and could even stay longer. If you can manage, I'll think up some excuse for Sally; perhaps hiking or something. But I'll leave that up to you. The longer we're together, the harder it will be to part. I'm getting hard just thinking of it. April 19th, hurry!

You check into tickets very soon, so that you qualify for a discount, and let me know your arrival time Thursday (evening?). I will try to synchronize. Maybe before I send this, I will get some tentative times. Good idea.

Dearest...

I can tell you are in a blue funk. And I am not helping you. I should have flooded you with letters to keep you company. But instead, I think how you must be feeling. I bet you feel the house is empty if Kit doesn't come. Well, you are so resilient. And there is always the telephone. However, I could and should have done more to make you happy.

You must be wondering why I haven't called you. First, Sally cancelled her trip. That cancelled the opportunity I was writing for. Then, I at least expected her to go out, some night. But she hasn't. So, I will have to make my excuses some night and come to my office. I will try to do that, next week.

I am glad to see you getting in with the *Advocate* group.
It sounds well-adjusted (despite the shenanigans on the bedroom
set!). You may even find Mr. Wright! If you do, it deserves me
wright. But I will be happy for you. I <u>do</u> want so much for you
to be happy and fulfilled. And now, more than ever, you need
someone to feel near to. I am not totally insensitive. I know.
Let me know how the *Advocate* experience goes. I read a
particularly obnoxious article in *Commentary* magazine, "Are
Homosexuals Gay?" It was so smug in its honky heterosexuality;
I almost wrote a letter to the editor. Because heterosexual
intercourse is natural in that the holes fit the plugs,
homosexuality must be unnatural! And homosexuals are deniers of
the passage to new generations! And so on and on. From one
piece of crap to another. A far cry from the piece I sent you.
You should turn the *Advocate* people loose on it.

I still have to get times for flights! If I hold up any
longer, I'll have to send you more money! All the money saver
seats will be reserved. I'll do it, tomorrow. Good night, my
love. I love you.

Finally, sweetheart, I have gotten some times, but they are
not certain. I can tell right now, synchronizing is not going
to be easy. Anyway, they will be trying to get me on a
Continental, arriving at 5:25 in Denver. But since I'm trying
to get a money saver seat (saving $125!), I will have to be
flexible.

I am not going to postpone mailing this any longer. I
haven't received anything from you in a week. So, I know you
are either angry with me for not writing sooner or more often,
or not calling, or you've fallen in love, or you are depressed
about Kit. I hope you are still seeing Nicky, frequently. I
wish the Denver trip were right now. I could be there to
comfort you, hold you in my arms. If you cried, I would kiss

away your tears. I would give you the love you want and deserve so much. Oh, Lynn. I wish I could you-know-what, but...

I have been under the weather, myself. Not sick. Just tired. I've skipped any swim several times, just because I've been so tired. I'm skipping it, right now. It may be a bug I'm fighting off. Or, it may be that I've lost some weight. Sally made some delicious homemade soups for supper, last week, and I may have lost about four pounds! (Which only brings me back down to the weight I was at when I was with you; Christmas was a disaster.) Anyway, I can even drink coffee and I still sleep like a log. I know it's not Spring fever. It snowed up a fury, yesterday. Lakes are still frozen.

Kisses to your luscious lips, my sweetheart. Don't delay getting a ticket.

Love,

Jim

A letter I wrote to Jim - Monday, March 12, 1979

My dearest James,

I'm deeply, deeply sorry for me, for you, and for us.

This will be my last letter, my darling, and I want to say exactly what is in my heart.

First, thank you for your love. When someone gives this most precious gift so freely and lavishly, one can only stand in awe.

I am so grateful for any part I played in focusing your love for your girls. I ran to my dear boys this evening for comfort; what rocks they are.

I want to say I'm sorry for giving the impression that there is only one responsible way to behave. You are the best judge of that for yourself, my dearest. You are a credit to your profession, a loyal friend, and a loving father. This is taking responsibility for your life! Forgive me for being so pushy and presumptuous in my last letter. I was swept away.

I won't forget you. How could I? Whenever I see the wildflowers on Mount Diablo, I'll think of you. Whenever I first see the Island Harbor around the bend, I'll think of you. In a hundred flashes, I'll see you; you are a part of me now, always.

But I must be responsible for my life. You told me all along what to expect and I chose not to believe it. I do now, my love. We must let go; to do otherwise would only lead to...
Evan and Anderson know.

So, my precious, I say goodbye not with any feeling of regret, but rather, an overwhelming appreciation for the human capacity to experience love and pain and to realize this is all part of being alive. Day will break and I'll go forth with a pocket full of seeds.

Lynn

Letter #10 – March 25, 1979

I won't say I've recovered from the shock yet, because the truth is I haven't. My first reaction was simply not to reply. But in your last note, you said you were miserable. Although I think you've overdone the "parting is such sweet sorrow" bit, I recognize a genuine tone which, curiously, makes me want to comfort you and strengthen you in your resolve, when what I should really do is kick you in the ass.

I do not understand why you are an either "sky's the limit or else nothing at all" type of person. But I am now convinced that you are. Given that fact, you are doing the right thing both for yourself and for me. It is certainly better that each of us lives without any hopes that depend on the other; better than each dashing the hopes of the other two pieces. I cannot satisfy your sky's the limit hopes, as I have explained time and time again, only to see your hopes rise anew to unrealizable levels. And you cannot, or at least believe you cannot, realize my hopes of meeting you again for an enjoyable weekend. So, I have had enough of disappointment from you and you have had enough of disappointment from me.

Remember Pandora's Box; the last and the worst thing to come from it was hope. My parting word to you is, beware your unrestrained hopes; they will make not just you, but those around you, miserable.

As for the future, what there was between us is still there, despite all this. I will think fondly of you often and, no doubt, will write to you, on occasion. You stick to your resolve and goddamit, go find your man! Which is what I've been saying since last March!

Love, despite all,

Jim

Letter #11 - September 12, 1979

Dear Lynn,

This is a letter of apology. I realize that if I want to cooperate with your decision, I should not disturb you by writing. But I have to make this one exception to apologize for the letter I wrote last. I can't bear that we part in anger. Please accept my apologies. In particular, it was stupid of me to suggest that your expectations of me were any less realistic than my expectations of you. And I apologize for any other stupid or hurtful remarks I made.

I hope you will cherish the memory of our love, just as I do. And I still do, very much. And I hope we can continue forever knowing that we each have a lasting, although distant and unattainable...friend. I owe you far more than I could ever say.

So, I will leave it at that. Best of luck to you and your kids, and whoever the lucky one is. And see the movie, "Les Folles du Cage" ("La Cage aux Folles"), if you haven't already. It had me in stitches. And I still laugh when I think of it a week later.

Love,

Jim

A message for you, the Tracker...

On March 12, 1979, I wrote a second breakup letter, twenty-five years after the first one to Jon. I concluded with the statement, "I'm going on with a pocket full of seeds." This phrase is the title of a book, written by my friend, Marilyn Sachs.

Well, after many plantings, none of those seeds germinated; probably my fault. Those wonderful guys had the misfortune of plowing after Jim. (For the life of me, who was G.F.?) So, the tracking back began, word by word...cards, notes, letters laid those tracks and by Christmas 1982, and those numerous sleepovers behind me, "Dearest" is once again my name. Who could resist?

So, Tracker, read on and follow the tracks.

Letter #12 – June 19, 1980

Dear Lynn,

It's about time that I sent you a newsy letter; I hope you agree. You probably thought of me during the news of the tornado. Well, I didn't even know about it until several weeks later. I was in Italy! It didn't come near our place, anyway.

The fact that I haven't written since last August does not mean I've forgotten you. Far from it! I think of you, always. But I think that you would prefer some "distance". I got your card informing me of "G.F." and I am happy for you. You deserve the fulfilling love you want so much and which you couldn't get from me. I'll admit that when I saw those initials, I felt sharp pangs of loss, as well as jealousy; the fires are still there. But, of course, I know better. And I do sincerely wish you both that deep, satisfying happiness that makes life worth living, and that comes from deep loving and being loved.

I and Sally spent four weeks in Italy. The kids went to my parents in Florida. It was magnificent; my first trip abroad! I remember you once commented that in Italy, men walked arm in arm. I wasn't prepared, however, for the physicality of male friendships. Truly beautiful. Arms around waists, around necks, kissing cheeks, rubbing and patting cheeks, even goosing!

We were in Rome ten days, Naples and Amalfi four, Florence eight, and Venice five. Food and art; art and food. My culinary discovery is a crusty melting Gorgonzola cheese, the likes of which I have never seen in the states. Excruciatingly delicious. The ten pounds I have on me over the weight you knew me by did not come only from indulging in Gorgonzola. I had to give up swimming for about three months because my legs became so excessively dry and oil-less from pool water chemicals that I developed an incredibly itchy rash.

You will not believe the prescription my doctor gave me for my legs. Rub them down every two hours with <u>Crisco</u>. He says it's the best skin oil there is. At first, I thought he was trying to tell me something. This guy knows the medical history of my penis and he once indicated that it suggested to him a proclivity to oral sex. I just kind of shook my head and muttered, "No, that's not it." Once, he gave me a sigmoidoscopy: a colon examination. I sweated and groaned, as he stuck the snake up there, enjoying every minute of it, secretly. After it was over, in about two minutes, he was truly amazed. He said it sometimes takes half an hour because people can't help pushing it out. And I let it in so easy. Well, I thought I had blown my cover, there. It reminded me of the time in San Francisco that a doctor put a wood stick on my tongue and asked me to say, "Ah." When my tongue offered no resistance to the entry of the stick, no gag response at all, he looked at me wide-eyed and said, "I can't do that." Whoops – cover blown, again.

Anyway, my legs now alternate between Nivea going into the pool and Crisco upon coming out. And I have just about gotten back to a half mile a day swimming. The ten pounds will come off over the next six weeks, while I am at Cornell University (Ithaca, New York), eating dormitory food. It is another philosophy summer institute, like the one I attended at Stanford. This time, I will be studying Ancient and Medieval Logic. (Incidentally, that essay I wrote and bragged about to you has finally found a publisher in one of the top five journals, if not the top one. But I had to cut thirty of my fifty pages! Oh, well. Better two-fifths published than not published at all.)

I have begun teaching Ancient Philosophy and together with the trip to Italy, I have become much better with the extraordinarily uninhibited homosexuality of ancient Greece. What a great time to live in. I had to explain this to my class because we were studying Plato's Symposium. I sweated for two weeks about how to approach it in a way that was true to my own self and yet, did not involve my coming screaming out of the closet, in front of everyone.

Well, I thought it went well, until one of my students came up afterwards and said, "Well, we've come a long way. Why just ten years ago, you couldn't have told the class that you've experienced homosexual love." I thought I had only confessed to "hero worship", while an adolescent. These kids know a euphemism when they hear one.

Anyway, I chat on and on. The male nude was the glory of ancient Greece and Roman copies found in the museums of Naples, Vatican, Capitoline, and those mainly are exquisite. They force you to look at the body with a sublimated eroticism which is hard to describe. It is as if your eyes could give you all the pleasure you could want from that body.

In Naples, their best nudes are those of Harmodias and Aristogeiton, the most famous pair of lovers in all Greece; one twenty years older than the other. And everywhere, there is Antinous, whose lover was the emperor Hadrian. His face influenced the nude Davids of Donatello and Michelangelo. And such a face!

And I discovered there was much more of a breaking out of, or disinhibiting of, the gay creative urge behind the Renaissance. Not only DaVinci and Michelangelo were gay but probably a century earlier, Donatello and Brunelleschi were, also. I can't help feeling that creative genius of the highest rank and homosexuality go together at a greater rate than you would expect from just pure chance.

I see that I have just rambled onto a fresh page. I seem
to recall that you were stationed in Italy, while in the Navy.
Is that right? Or, was it that you never were on duty on a
ship, just stayed in that boarding house in Virginia?

Someday, next winter, when it is cold and rainy, sit down
and surprise me with a newsy letter. Tell me about G.F. Tell
me about Kit and Nicky. How has Kit's military career
progressed? Do you see them as much as you used to? That was
in the process of changing, as our letters broke off. Then,
there was EST. A few months ago, I was in a bar in Detroit and
a young kid sits down beside me, brimming over with happiness.
It wasn't long before it spilled over into talk; to
anyone...bartender, people all around. Since I was the most
convenient, he settled into a long conversation with me. It
turned out that his buoyant happiness was the product of his EST
seminar of just a few months before. I have seen and talked to
people like him, before. But they were experiencing the effects
of a religious conversion. Mr. Erhard seems to have the
capacity of filling people with the Holy Spirit, without either
he or they being aware of it. However, I have not myself
entered the fold, although this fellow made a very good pitch
for it.

And if you don't write, I'll understand. And if you don't
want me to write, let me know and I'll understand. (I'm so
goddam understanding.) But if you do write, wait 'til after
September, since I'll be away 'til then. For after my
"philosophy camp", we are all off tenting for two weeks up to
Winnipeg, where Sally has a conference. I and the girls will
find some lake. They are nine (to be ten in November) and
seven. Emma will be taking horse riding lessons, this summer.
Yesterday, I took her to see, "The Black Stallion". Excellent!

Do I remember right that Kit knows Francis Ford Coppola? Alice refused to go. Her girlfriend told her about the fire on the ship. Then, visits to family in Chicago and then, back to the grind. Back to filling the coffers.

Someday, I'll make it back to S.F. I hope if I ever do, we could meet again...both of you.

And Happy Birthday! (July 14th?)

Love & Kisses (just a few pecks),

Jim

Letter #13 — December 18, 1981

Dear Lynn,

The last day of school, and me swearing I will find time to write to you, and what to my wondering eyes doth appear, but a Christmas card from you! So, that settled it. Let the goddam exams wait. I'm writing to the man I love; yes, still. I think of you, very often; recently, with some guilt about not writing sooner. It's interesting that you should comment that you are fine and I hoped your last letter didn't worry me. It's true that I did not want to write back <u>too</u> soon, if you were between lovers. Because I didn't want to...oh, hell, you know. But I did start writing in May and I still have some of that letter at home. But it was going to be a very long letter and so, of course, it never got finished.

Anyway, I enjoyed your letter very much, and your card, and the photo of you as Lady Bright...a tragic hero if ever I saw one...and both photographs, especially the second one with your shirt hanging open, reminds me of your hairy chest. Yummy. And that other handsome stud next to you. Well, anytime he appears as a centerfold in Playgirl, please let me know. Kit is maturing into a stunningly handsome fellow. But of course, look at his Dad.

I remember reflecting after your breakup with G.F. that the most constant thing in your life since your divorce is still your family. It's great that you have been able to keep that.

As for me, I have just completed one of the busiest terms I've ever had. Believe it or not, I taught a college mathematics course: matrix algebra, linear programming, probability theory, and statistics! What an experience, having forty students looking over your shoulders, as you fumble around with fractions and negative numbers for the first time in 25 years. The reason for this is the godawful state of the

Michigan economy. The math department couldn't afford to hire part timers. More recently, the administration has started to close down programs; librarianship for me. Sally's department, religion, will lose its Masters and, if the VP gets its way, it's major. Philosophy has been asked to put one of us on alternate year appointment, to teach in the Spring and Summer. So, no extra pay possibilities, anymore. Everybody realizes that if this money squeeze continues, there will be many layoffs. And not only is the money crunch continuing, but we are about to hit the population decline at the college level, in a year or two. So much for tenure and security.

And as for my sex life, it is entirely within the bounds of matrimony. I did proposition a pretty young thing standing around naked in our clubhouse. But he had to refuse, since he has three lovers, one a girl, who are paying his way and he can't afford to complicate such tidy arrangements. So, I kissed his shoulder and asked him to put me on his waiting list. I should have given him a hickey.

And a few weeks ago, I got a letter from "a friend of a friend", who will be coming to town for a meeting in March. Perhaps something will come of that. He is married and asks how do I cope. So, I'm expecting heavy therapy sessions. I hope we can squeeze some sex in.

Oh, I wish I were there with you. What a good time we had, together...kissing, hugging, loving. We were great bed companions; look what pictures of your hairy chest do to me! I'm getting horny.

I know you are wondering why I haven't been to S.F. in these past two years. So am I! But it isn't easy to: A) get on convention programs; B) get a school to fund travel that far away. But I haven't given up trying and I will call you, when I do. (Do you know that before your last letter, I wasn't sure you

would want me to?) The craziest thing is that when I finish
this note, I am going to a goodbye party for a fellow who has
taken a temporary union job for the AAUP in S.F.! And I founded
the union, here, and he was one of my proteges, and he gets the
job (which I didn't even know about).

Do you remember Doug Jones? We had drinks with him, once.
He's called me twice. Once last year, after he had another
severe heart attack, and once this Fall, while visiting his
mother, here. HE survives but his heart is about to give out.
He told me that he was honored at a big banquet by the Society
of Gerontologists. Not only for his services in gerontology but
also in gay liberation. And sometime this Fall, *The Advocate*
printed an interview with him. Perhaps you saw it; I didn't. A
great man, <u>really</u>.

Kiss all my friends hello for me, but most of all, close
your eyes and imagine I am lying next to you, because in spirit,
I am.

Love,

Jim

Letter #14 – May 28, 1982

My dearest,

    You've done it, again; beat me to it. I guess I shall always be a lousy letter writer; I always have been. But I was going to write to you before the end of next week, when I go on another summer seminar; alas, to Cornell, again. The director is emerita from UC Davis. So, why did she have to locate it in New York?

    Your card was SO RIGHT! SO PERFECT!! Just when I had begun to think my hormonal levels had gone down to empty, I open your card and swoosh! Androgens, testosterone, the whole works come flowing up. I often think how beautiful a society would be where men and boys could show such physical affection, when it seems to be so natural to feel it. It was that way in ancient Greece. I have it here in front of me, as I write. I've been using it as a book mark; hardly get any reading done!

    How I would like to lie beside you and just run my hands through your hair and to reaffirm our familiarity with each other's body by casual caresses. I think of you, <u>always</u>. I am <u>always</u> writing to you, in my mind. I just never get around to sending them, that's all. But today, I am all alone celebrating my forty-four thousandth birthday. So, I am going to spend it with you. (Sally is off to Harvard for four days; kids in school.)

    Just think...we haven't seen each other in four-thousand years (minus two-thousand weeks). How have you changed? From your pictures, not at all. I am about the same, too, except I have watched my weight creep up, slowly. I am now thirteen pounds heavier than when we were together. I have been trying to get it down, but it's going to take some real hunger to do it. I blame it on Sarkozy's Bakery; a bread bakery which is incredibly good. Then, there's wine and my sweet tooth. They

are there when I least suspect it and my defenses are down.
Like last night...I take my kids to the school art fair and
wouldn't you know, the PTA is selling chocolate brownies. So,
after my supper of Stouffers Slim Gourmet chicken and rice at
less than 300 calories, I eat two chocolate brownies. And so it
goes. But it is a serious matter, once I go over 170. Namely,
$500 of suits and pants in my closet become useless. My tailor
let out my pants of my best suit and warned that's as far as it
will go. So, I must, I will, I shall, I hope. Why can't I be
with you and eat rabbit food twice a week?

So, you are dating a Greek active? I'm jealous. Shall I
tell you about my spree with a Greek active? He was only 18
years old and in fact, was in my class. We got to talking about
things and he invited me over to his house. When I saw the nude
hung up on the bathroom wall, it was obvious that he and the
ones he shared the house with had similar tastes. He told me
they were a group of guys who had a lot in common. Being Greek
and active was apparently one of them. Well, I showed that I
approved, heartily. So, we spent a very enjoyable hour or so,
together. I forgot the name of the fraternity, Sigma something
or other. Being active means living in the frat house, as
opposed to being a member but living outside. And the nude in
the bathroom had exceptionally large tits. Ho hum.

I believe I mentioned that I scheduled a date with a
visiting professor. Well, nothing came of that, either. We
exchanged some letters, but when the day arrived for his
arrival, he called and pleaded financial crisis at his
university, etc., etc. Of course, I knew what was on his mind;
first night jitters. So, I have halitosis, crabs, syphilis,
gonorrhea, 300 pounds of flab, and want to do all the things he
doesn't, etc.? He's married, too. In fact, he just recently
remarried, which I cannot fathom, at all.

I would much rather be with you, anyway. About a week ago, I was looking over a bunch of bananas and picked out what seemed to be an exceptionally thick one. I peeled it and as I slipped it into my mouth, I had this strange déjà vu feeling, so that instead of biting it, I kept on pushing it in, until my mouth was full and then, I remembered your thick, wonderfully mouth-filling cock. Of course, your cock has it all over bananas for smoothness and excitement.

Do you know what the picture card reminds me of? Our trip together to Mount Diablo. We were climbing around rocks and sat down together for lunch. Those were lovely moments; moments of love that I'll never forget. Without you, I would never have become a complete person. Thank you, Lynn, my lover! My beloved! We SHALL get together, again. I only wish I knew when.

In three years, we come up for sabbaticals, again. But it seems that the two most likely relocation spots are Sri Lanka or Cambridge, England, if there are still jobs and sabbaticals, then. This year, my department had: 1) its Chairman reduced to academic year, from fiscal year; 2) its secretary reduced to half time; 3) the opportunities for summer teaching eliminated by having faculty teach them as part of their regular load; 4) three faculty members teach high-demand courses outside the department, including yours truly, which I will be doing again, next year. If there are any more financial cuts, I'm afraid it will be firings. If Chrysler goes under, and it still could, the ripples might capsize us.

But in the meantime, I spade up my salad garden, cut flowers...we are in mid-iris season, now...with the peonies due in a day or two, and watch birds. A pair of mourning doves coo outside my study, as I work through population genetics. My summer seminar is on the philosophy of biology; as best I can,

considering the distracting book I use. A robin has built its
nest within three feet of our living room windows. Then, in the
evening, I read Peter Wimsey mysteries or Dickens, feeling
desperately hungry, all the while, and thinking of you, as
always. Thank you for the beautiful card and have yourself a
great birthday...Bastille Day, too. I shall be thinking of you
in Ithaca.

    Love and endless kisses,

    Jim

Letter #15 – December 9, 1982

And a ho-ho-ho; here I am, again. The picture which you have or will find is to remind you how ugly I am. The photographer caught me in a moment of indecision about whether to frown or smile. I had the picture taken to accompany my acceptance of an invitation to attend "the eleventh ICUS" conference in Philadelphia, over Thanksgiving weekend which, in case you haven't heard, is the infamous international get-together of intellectuals, sponsored by the second person of the blessed Trinity, and his charming wife, the third person of the blessed Trinity, none other than the Reverend Sun Myung Moon. It's supposed to be bad form to accept the hospitality of, and lend credibility to, what many consider a front for Right Wing political activity. But my curiosity got the better of me and I ended up enjoying myself immensely, and as for being brainwashed in the process...well, I manage to sell my quota of roses early enough, so that I don't miss my classes. Incidentally, an interesting and well-written book by an ex-Moonie, which you'd like and would be good for school libraries, is Steven Kemperman's, *Lord of the Second Advent*, now in paper(back). I use it in my Logic classes.

OK. You see how my letters wander. I imagine I'm sitting with you over soup and salad and talking a blue streak with you. How I miss those days, five years ago! Bad news. The Pacific division of the American Philosophical Association is meeting at the Claremont which, if I remember correctly, is the white hotel up the hill from you...in March, first week. But I'd have to be on the program in order to come, and I'm virtually certain that I didn't make it, since I would have been informed by now, if I had. I even had a $400 subsidy lined up, but it was contingent on getting on the program. Pardon my expression, but shit! We seem destined to not meet again, it almost seems, although I refuse to believe it.

The last time I wrote was before my trip to Cornell. That was interesting, too; learned a few things, made some new friends, one of whom is interested in co-editing a book with me, and lost some unnecessary pounds. I now fit in my clothes, again. But alas, the period from Halloween, when I do my duty of sampling my kids' take, through Emma's birthday, through gift fruitcakes (today's temptation), Thanksgiving and Christmas pig-outs, etc., is here. So far, I'm holding my own.

Cornell was fun in another way. They have a "men only" hour in the gym pool. (Pen ran out.) And no bathing suit is required. Unfortunately, most guys use their suits, anyway. However, there were enough of us free spirits to make it interesting. We would enjoy the feeling of streams of water running through our pubic hair and as we reached the end of a lap, there under the water to greet us was another little brother, floating in a bed of pubic hair. The turn-ons continued right into the shower stalls, where things got so kinky sometimes that I actually got hard twice without a stitch of embarrassment. Others were doing it, too! It's great to be off in a place where you are anonymous and can be natural; not like my own pool, here. There's plenty of activity, but not for me. Anyway, although it never got beyond mutual "showings", it proved there's life in the old bone, yet.

And how's your bone? Are you still between lovers? I hope not. I hope your dreams are fulfilled, because they're mine, too, and I'd like at least one of us to fulfill them, and I know I won't. I still love you, you know. I still make love to you in my fantasies. But that's for me. You should have the real thing, and I hope you have found it, again.

And I hope Kit is off in West Point. I know that was his dream. Wish him a Merry Christmas for me, if he has any memory of me; and Nick, too. And for you, what can I say? XXXXXXX. Can we send kisses by ESP? I had my students try their ESP powers on cards. No one did better than what had a 10% probability of occurring by coincidence. I'm still teaching math, too.

Love and many kisses,

Jim

Oh, for five minutes under the mistletoe with you...!

Letter #16 – May 25, 1983

Dear Lynn,

I am ashamed of myself. It's five months since I've written and since I learned of your bout with hepatitis. Despite your assuring me not to worry about you, I have. In fact, there's one consolation in my not writing. The longer I put it off, the more I think of you. For the last month, you've been the subject of my thoughts almost hourly. Don't think I'm callous for not writing. I do worry about you. I was alarmed by your long period of convalescence: three months! I was alarmed when I learned that hepatitis B carriers are most susceptible to AIDS, which is one of the worst things I've heard about, recently. And its incidence is doubling every six months, they say. So, do take care of yourself. Stay out of the baths and stick with that priest.

You can tell him for me that when I was a boy, I wanted to be an altar boy, first to wear the cassock, then after puberty, to go back into the sacristy and to have a love affair with a priest. First, the love affairs of my fantasies were very platonic. As I got older, they became less so. Unfortunately, it always stayed fantasy. I was never propositioned by a priest. Darn.

I have committed very few indiscretions (as they say) to entertain you with. When in Chicago, I did attend a Gay Film Festival showing of the most outrageous, most campy, flick I've ever seen. A San Francisco filmmaker, whose name escapes me; McDonald? No. McDowell? No. Mostly straight sex, once between a man and a gorilla. After that, I went out for some honest-to-goodness porn, filmed by a guy named Higgins. There was a lot of traffic into the back room of the theater. So naturally, I had to look. It wasn't five minutes before some guy ten years younger than me had me standing on a platform, while he gave me one of the most delicious sucks I have ever experienced. I must say, the most professional suckers are in Chicago, at least in my experience.

Part of my inactivity comes from fear of disease, I suppose. There are bacteria which bother women more than men. Haemophilus is one. Sally and I had to take ampicillin to get rid of that. It is spread through oral sex. Since I never "oral" Sally, she must have wondered. I hope I didn't reacquire Haemophilus in Chicago.

I saw an ad in *The Advocate* from a 23-year-old bodybuilder, looking for a sugar daddy. "Must be very generous." He lived in Kalamazoo. So, I wrote him a letter, telling no lies, including that I would not pay his rent. Nothing came of it, as could be expected. Then, at one place where I said I'd be, I ran into a doctor neighbor of mine, who acted somewhat nervous, like a straight walking into a gay bar for the first time. Then, it hit me. Could the ad have been a plant; a joke by a group of doctors to decloset friends and neighbors for laughs??

By the time you get this, I'll be 45...tralala. Five years since my party at your place. I still remember one of my dumbest tricks, preventing my birthday cake from falling from my car seat to the floor by slamming my hand down on the top of the cake box…

Back from lunch. Our computer class took our instructor to lunch. Yes, I've decided to succumb to the computer revolution. I've even developed a callus on my middle finger from the keyboard on my terminal. I haven't bought one, but I have a terminal that hooks up to the school's.

I should have written to tell you I love you. I'm sorry for the delay. I loved your Valentines card. I loved your pen, too. Silver ink which bleeds a red border. Really, now!

But that's one of the reasons I love you. You do things like that. The other reasons are your kisses, your smile, your upbeat personality, your handsome looks, your manly five o'clock shadow, hair that thrills the finger tips, body that thrills the other tip, etc. We SHALL get together.

But in the meantime, I'm off to Boston with the family. I've never been to Boston. Sally finagled a free apartment at Harvard, for June. Then, up the coast to Maine, perhaps the Bay of Fundy, eating seafood all the way. Then, home to the garden going to weeds. I hope your weather has returned to normal. Thank you for the loan of your California weather, this winter. We normally have foot snow cover continuously from the middle of December to the middle of March. This year, the first real snow didn't even come until March 21st! The blackberries and raspberries will be fantastic this summer because normally, the rabbits eat the canes back to the snow line each winter and this year, they were left untouched. They also say the mosquitoes will be fantastic this year. Swimming, gardening, and thinking; what a life. Four months not teaching. But there is this emptiness which didn't exist when I was near you. I can't tell you how blah it all can be, when you are not with the one you love. One scheme that crossed my mind is for me to arrange to get you on the invitation list to Moonie conventions. I mentioned that I had gone to one in Philadelphia. But they also invite me to other purely religious indoctrination seminars. So far, I have not gone to any. I've turned down a week, all-expenses paid, in: Acapulco; Seoul; Jamaica. Perhaps I can figure out a way for us to honeymoon at the Rev. Moon's expense.

Sabbatical year is coming up again, '84 – '85. Sally is applying for a fellowship to India, and perhaps I will, too. If we go only for a part of the year, the rest will probably be spent in Cambridge, England. I would like the kids to

experience living in a foreign land. I never did. In fact, the
first trip I ever took was a few years ago, to Italy. That was
the year you were tricking in a burnoose in Morocco. That's
actually better than tricking in a cassock in the sacristy!

I suppose if I were to suggest sabbaticaling again in San
Francisco, if current plans fell through, I might be able to
pull it off. But we shall see.

One possibility is that I will get laid off. (How's that
for a visual pun?) Higher ed. in this state is in shambles,
between money troubles and declining student enrollment. Sally
is second from the bottom in her department. And the bottom man
just got his layoff notice. Now, Sally is last and word has it
that they are going to slash another $3 million worth for the
following year. I'm three in my department of seven, which is
safe, I suppose, unless they decide they can do without a
Philosophy department. We just got rid of another VP...in
effect, chancellor...who had that in mind. If you read Mary
McCarthy's *Groves of Academe*, it was something like that. The
Veep was extraordinarily indiscreet in his choice of language in
a memo. The memo happened to reach the hands of one of the
people he had just laid off, who then xeroxed the memo and
circulated widely. It incensed the faculty. There was a big
Faculty Senate meeting. The Veep eventually lost his cool
entirely and reportedly started shouting at the President for
not supporting him. The President fired him on the spot.

This is something of a replay of my days in unionizing,
here. I also went after a VP and got him. I recently learned
that guy has been fired again from Hilo, Hawaii in another
replay of, *Grove of Academe*. He denied tenure to a Hawaiian
native who was well connected in the state legislature.
Goodbye, VP. The native is still on the faculty. Oh, I just

love it when bureaucrats get their heads handed to them! But enough.

You are, I firmly hope, fully recovered and enjoying yourself, with an immune lover. I promise to get immunized as soon as there's a chance we might meet. After all, I don't want to have to put a condom on my tongue to French kiss you; or a condom anywhere else, for that matter.

Take care, love.

Jim

Letter #17 - December 25, 1983

Dear Lynn,

I didn't have any writing paper handy. So, I just grabbed the Sunday *New York Times* and tore a piece out at random, as you can see. I hope you don't mind my flashing off a letter on such scrap.

Things have been happening. Our sabbaticals came through and...smooch, smooch...we both stand very good chances of winning Company Fellowships to INDIA, of all places! We both have been officially nominated by US to India. I won't know for sure if India accepts until April. But it's likely. One hitch: I applied to teach in Calcutta; Sally has applied for New Delhi. If we both get fellowships, I might live in Calcutta with just my all-male household. It's a town that's two-thirds male and boys must be a dime a dozen. At least, I hope so. Do you know anyone who knows the scene in Calcutta? If so, let me know what you find out. How does one get a gay cook, for example? Now this is odd. I seem to be getting an erection. I hope you are, too.

Merry Christmas, my love. Or, since this will probably arrive after Christmas, considering the male...I mean the mail...Happy New Year! Your last letter made me very happy. You sound so serene and happy, yourself. I would have sent for the books you mentioned, belly button; I'm such a rationalist, they most likely wouldn't have affected me as they did you. You, but not the books, could always get to me. Not only physically. Your enthusiasm always thrills me. How's your erection? Oh, cum, all ye Christmas Day, man. Slurp, slurp. I miss you very much. I feel lonely, most of the time. I need to love you at close quarters.

And let's see, something else has entered my life: my own microcomputer. I just bought a "DEC Rainbow" at half price,

new, and I'm waiting for delivery, right now. I've become an
avid word processor. And I'll dabble in programming in Pascal,
a computer language. Gee, I forgot to bite that ear on the way
down the page. Have you noticed how many guys wear diamonds in
their ears now, even in the Midwest? Well, let's give 'em a
hickey or two on the neck.
When all the extras are bought...programs, printer, modem, etc.,
I expect to have spent about $4,000!! I wonder if anyone has
written an adventure game for the computer with us in mind.
Someone in S.F. must have. But, of course, they are not
advertised in *Byte* magazine. If you've heard of any such
programs, let me know. I do it all vicariously now, anyway.
And I'll need some relief from writing the book I promised for
my sabbatical. Speaking of *Byte*, should we give this nipple a
couple of Bytes? The book will be on fate, the same as my last
sabbatical. But in the meantime, I've published seven articles
on or near the topic. So, I've decided it's time to try a book.
We shall see.

How would you like this heavily veined and hairy hand
wrapped around your cock? Maybe the book I write on my $4,000
word processor should be a sex fantasy. Probably sell better
than a dry book on fate.

I hope your handsome sons are doing well. How's Kit
enjoying the real thing? And how old is Nicky, now? And is he
too straight? I suppose you'll have to reconcile yourself to
being a grandpa, soon, many times over. There's a fullness in
family life that I'd miss if I didn't have it. I only wish I
had the kind of love that comes most naturally to me, too. How
are you doing in that quarter? If I had any hope of seeing you
soon, I would have gotten my shots; and I will, as soon as I
know there is a chance. My guess is that you are as rock hard
now, as I am. How would you like to explore the interior of

these gorgeous buns? They certainly do more for me than The
Maidenform Woman. Here's wrapping my arms close around you,
closing my eyes, and putting my lips to yours, as you said on
your card...forever.

    Love,

    Jim

Letter #18 – June 6, 1984

Dearest Lynn,

I love you!! "XXXXX." I came into the office today to write you a letter and there was yours in my mailbox. I only read your poem on "self-pleasuring", so far. But let's admit it. How much better it was when we were in each other's arms. Now, I'll read your letter…

How you do remember detail! You're right. I was as crushed as the cake was. And your reaction DID relieve me, so much!!

Oh, God. Did I confess to fifteen extra pounds? I wasn't going to mention it, this time. But it's coming off, soon. And by the way, I've been much more attentive to my fingernails, since you mentioned it in your last letter.

I heard about that S.F. ordinance. No sex in S.F. baths!! I have to get protection from hepatitis for my trip to India; more on that, later. I asked my doctor about B-vaccine. He called Atlanta and later told me it costs $100. Furthermore, it is neither recommended nor not recommended. But I must get gamma globulin for A Hepatitis.

Nonsense. I never felt you were "intellectually lacking". Honestly now, there was never any such feeling in our relationship, was there? I know I never felt it.

Shit on Carl. But all chicken-chasers get their punishment. To paraphrase Oscar Wilde: chicken always kills the thing it loves.

Enjoy Dick. To hell with chemistry. There are many kinds of delights that come from friendship. Cultivate Fabian, Bob, Bob D., etc. (Did I just say, "Enjoy dick,"? Must be Freudian.)

And now you ask my plans. Here they are: tomorrow morning, 7:30, fly to Florida with girls for week with parents, Epcot, Cape Kennedy. Sally stays home to teach. I'm off.

As soon as I return, I'm off to Rochester, New York: University of Rochester. In a moment of self-doubt about getting a Company to India, I applied for a National Endowment for the Humanities summer seminar on Inductive Logic and the Philosophy of Science. Then, I got both! So, there in Rochester I'll be to August 10th...all alone.

Then, I fly directly from Rochester to India, meeting family in N.Y. I will be at Jadavpur University in Calcutta, until May 15, 1985. Again, all alone, because Sally won a Company, too. Two in one family; quite unusual. Hers is in New Delhi. Children will stay with her.

My current tentative plan is to stay at the Ramakrishna Missions International Guest House, in Calcutta. Perhaps I'll pick up some Vedanta. Who knows? Just so long as I don't pick up any social diseases.

You were right in your earlier letter about fantasy vs. reality, as in your Mexico City experience. I would be in an especially vulnerable position, precisely because of the difference in economics between me and, say, possible tricks.

India seems to make Western men go sexually dormant. Not women, it seems; I just saw, "Heat and Dust", a week ago. But I can still have my fantasies. One of them is that you come to stay with me. Unlike "Heat and Dust" scenery, Calcutta is green and lush. Unfortunately, the humidity is a constant 80% to 90%, year-round! Think you can handle it...lying there in bed under the mosquito netting, not being able to sleep for the heat? What would we do? (What wouldn't we do?)

As soon as I know my mailing addresses in Rochester and in Calcutta, I will write again. In fact, I will write to you more than this miserable twice a year. You are in my thoughts CONSTANTLY as the one person with whom I have felt so whole, so fulfilled, so happy in the fullest sense. I miss you terribly. We are <u>intimate</u>; it's the word that expresses for me the kind of relationship that gives meaning to my life.

There's a very beautiful book, Edmund White's *Nocturnes for the King of Naples*. It's about an ex-chicken looking back on his life with his lover and discovering, too late, that it was the relationship that gave his life meaning. Oh, read it! It's as beautiful as poetry (not porn). It's published in Penguin Paperbacks.

I love you more and more…

Jim

Letter #19 – June 19, 1984

Dear Lover,

I ring the outside door. The buzzer is heard and I open and press the elevator button: open. I go in and press "3". Up, and open, again. I turn right, to the end of the hall; 305. I turn the knob. It opens.

And there you are, across from the door, weight shifted to one leg, framed by the kitchen archway. Beautiful eyes, eying your meat course for the night and sending thrills straight into my groin. Your beautiful, wide smile...how I love it! Making me smile, too.

I will never forget how we would kiss. Arms enfolding me; my arms around you. Then, our lips would touch gently, then press. Not fast, not forced, but as it worked on us. As I began to get hard, our lips would open and tongues would meet. I'm getting hard, right now. Oh! It was always so good, Lynn! I always liked to feel the feel of your lips on mine. They're so sensuous. Your lips are my erogenous zone. How long were our kisses! We would lose ourselves in each other, making our union forever. I felt that way. And everything else we'd do that day was just a celebration of the union we had formed with our first kiss. *sigh*

I often go over our lovemaking in bed, step by step, like this. But that is too long, for now. And besides, that's my masturbation fantasy. I wouldn't get much writing done. But I'll just say, your glans was a miracle of beauty. Bigger than mine. How I loved the feel of it in my mouth, tonguing it from the hole down the crease underside and then, rubbing it and greasing up your balls, waiting for you to scream as I massaged them. Oh, what the hell. I wasn't going to wank off, tonight. But why not. So, here is my Nivea all over my cock and yours. I'm going to...no, you're going to, come with my cock up your ass...whoops...Nivea getting on paper. Oh...you're sitting on my cock and rubbing my nipples with cream and I'm squeezing your balls and licking on your marvelous dick; then, creaming it over and feeling it get rock hard. I open my mouth as a bull's eye for your squirt. I tease the hole with my tongue. And then, as you release your cream, I stop and you fall down on top of me in exhaustion. (I just came!)

I'd just hold you in my arms, just feeling your sexual release, as if it were my own. *sigh*

Anyway, here I am in Rochester, N.Y., 'til the first week in August. There's ten gay bars, here, and a bath. I wish there were a gay movie house, because it's less risky. I'll just have to avoid the riskier form of contact. Probably, I'll avoid all. *sigh*

I'm in a dorm, here. I think there's a suite of girls, who have been taking acid together, from the screams, hysterical laughter, and crying I'm hearing. It's 12:45 at night!

My address, here, is: PO Box A3000; Creek Station; Rochester, New York; 14650.

I visited Epcot and NASA, while in Florida. I really enjoyed it all. At the Japanese Pavilion restaurant, I impressed all, when they handed out hot cloths to wipe our hands with. When I returned mine, it spelled, "Good luck," in Japanese. I accomplished these marks by carefully working the cloth under each of my fingernails.

Love and huge kisses,

Jim

P.S.: Anyone in S.F. have a recipe for curried semen? I know you and Nick will have a great time. I took out the picture of you and Kit with Alhambra behind you, just before coming out here. Gee, you two were handsome, and I'll bet Nick is, too. Send me at least a postcard!

Letter #20 – June 27, 1984

Dearest Lynn,

I feel all jittery, like a virgin giving in for the first time. The first thing I did was schedule my first Hep B shot, for 9:15, this Monday (July 2nd). Booster comes first week of August. Wow! After seven years, I'd sort of given up on our getting together, again. Now, the thrill has taken my breath away! I'm getting constant elongations. My balls are in constant motion; up and down in the pouch! I'll have to add a few more laps in my schedule, to shape up. Give up beer and desserts.

My feeling about timing is:

    1. The longer your stay, the better;

    2. The sooner you come, the better.

Besides Christmas and Easter, I'll probably be with my family in New Delhi. They will most likely visit me in October, when Calcutta has a big religious holiday.

Lynn, my love. Have you checked cost? It's likely to cost you nearly $2,000! But if that's okay, I promise to do everything with you for that three weeks. The "mountains" you list could be either Himalayas...we'd go to Darjeeling, or further south in Orissa. We'd go to beaches there, too. The undertow is so strong there, we'd each have our personal lifeguard. (I've fantasized about getting picked up, there...or picking up.)

You might be interested in a book, *Days and Nights in Calcutta*, by Blaise and Mukherjee...husband and wife...who recorded their year-long stay, as a joint diary. Mukherjee...her first name escapes me but she's a novelist...also went to Loretto Convent as, indeed, all the up and coming girls of Calcutta did. They also stayed at the

Ramakrishna Mission International Guest House, Ballygunge, Gol Park, in Calcutta. That is where I've requested to stay.

Here are all the things that are still uncertain, that could foul up our timing:

1. Since I'm going for almost ten months, I have to get what is called an "entry" visa. You'd get a tourist visa and there's no problem, there. But mine is difficult to get. It has happened that people have been delayed for several months. My request went in a month ago and I still don't have it;

2. I go by Pan Am from New York to Frankfurt to New Delhi. I don't have the exact...oh, I must, I'll look again...can't find it. But I leave N.Y. sometime between four and eight on Friday, August 10th, arrive in Frankfurt about morning with a four-hour stopover, then on to New Delhi, arriving at 2AM in the morning, August 12th (having lost 9½ hours). Then, I stay in New Delhi for a few days, getting oriented by the Company people;

3. How long is an if? August 15th is Independence Day in India. So, I'm not sure if I'll arrive in Calcutta on the 15th or 16th;

4. Where I'll be staying is still open. The Company people arrange that, although I requested the Ramakrishna Mission, which is said to be clean, reasonable, and sort of air conditioned, if the power is on (which in Calcutta is a very big if). Perhaps you can be a guest in my room, while you're there, if I'm there. Would that be okay with you? (Just joking.);

5. My duties at Jadavpur are still up in the air, nothing settled, although I am supposed to spend six hours a week teaching there. The department also has many workshops for faculty that I may be expected to attend. I have no way of knowing, now. But usually, obligations are very light at the

beginning of a stay and tend to pile up, as time passes. So,
from that point of view, August is good;

      6. I doubt that it will happen, but it's conceivable
that Sally will come with me for a visit. But I think she'll
postpone that until October.

      I will have two hepatitis shots, by then. Will that give
me full immunity for the time we're together? Even if not full,
nothing would keep me from making love with you, once we're
together! You will want shots, too. Recommended are:
tetanus/diphtheria; typhoid (with booster); cholera (with
booster); gamma globulin, first, before you go...that's for
Hepatitis A. I don't know if the risk is that great during a
three week stay. You might check that. In addition, I got a
polio booster and a tuberculin skin test for before; after-test
to pinpoint time of contraction if the after-test is positive…
Whoops – time for a swim!

      Back. Elongated all the way there; elongated in the
shower. Oh! But I'll save it for tonight. I haven't been
quite celibate this past week and a half, as my last letter's
Nivea smear showed. I've gone to the baths three times, but no
fluid exchanges. Really, just to watch the porn. But I'll have
to be careful, since temptation does mount. The first night,
four guys got to feeling my hardon, as I watched. When one of
them told me of a good fuck in room 30, I went. Luckily, the
door was locked, so I went home, instead. Second time, I let a
hairy armed guy suck me. But what he called sucking I wouldn't
wish on a kielbasa. So, I didn't come. The third time was
really tempting. A small, young muscle builder, lying in his
room, door open. He'd just been sucked. So, he said he was
resting. Second time visited, he was on his stomach, so I felt
up his ass. Third time, he's standing outside his door and
signals for me to feel him up, which I did. But he didn't get

turned on. Half hour later, he's lying in his room, door open, slowly jacking off. So, not wanting to be rejected again, I stuck just my dick inside his door. All he could see was this dick jacking off. I peeked and he was watching, jacking off harder. So, I went in dropped my towel and started jacking off, but good. He said, "Holy shit!," staring at my penis, which had gotten too swollen for my short foreskin to go over it. And he got up to play with it, or suck it. Then, a funny thing happened before he touched it: I came. The poor guy looked so disappointed, and so was I. So, he just bug-eyed me coming, as I bug-eyed his beautiful, tight, little body. Then, he decided he should leave "before I do something to hurt myself", as he said, probably meaning taking fluids. So, we showered together and went our separate ways. I'm wondering what will happen if I meet up with him, again? Even at age forty-six, at any one time in the baths, I'd be the third or fourth best-looking guy, there. And with my universally admired cock, I seem to have an entrée anywhere! How's that for conceited, bragging narcissism?

I also attend a Dignity/Integrity service, Sunday. Integrity is Episcopal, Dignity is Catholic. Every fourth service is Episcopal. It was quite moving; the first time I've taken communion in almost twenty years. Afterwards, nine of us, including two women, went for supper. I don't really understand these people but I felt their welcome as generous and sincere. Also, the big Italian buck I sat across from, with forearms as big as my calves, began to charm me too much; and perhaps me, him. That's why I went to the baths a third time; to get him out of my system. Anyway, I go back, next Sunday. Maybe I'll recover my faith if I can really come to believe that God is love, as Saint John said. If God is love, let him love me through a community of homosexuals. Only then will I feel the freedom and peace to love others as God loves me.

I'm now going to run to the shoe store to get new heels.

It occurs to me that there's a Ramakrishna Mission in San Francisco. They may be able to tell you the rules about the International Guest House. It may not be for short term or for people who bill themselves as "tourists". I also know that the organizer of "San Francisco Sidewalk Astronomers" is associated with this group. But I forgot his name.

Writing to you has made me feel a bit guilty. I have yet to write to my children, although I've spoken to Sally on the phone, several times. That's what I'll do, tonight. Emma is thirteen, and a very pretty young lady. Alice is just eleven and having the weight problem Nicky had, seven years ago. But she's pretty, nevertheless. I went to a gay parents meeting, here, but it was a fizzle. The facilitator and one other showed. They were both women and it was quite interesting to hear them both speculating that their teenage sons were gay. One was out to her children, one wasn't. I know my children are straight, judging from all the beautiful faces pinned up all over their rooms (not just Michael Jackson). I can't wait until they graduate from teeny bopper magazines to Playgirl.

Which reminds me....*Advocate's* new mag, *Men*, is quite good. Except you didn't seem to go for pinup mags.

As you can see, I can go on and on and on, just as we did over our wine and soup and salad, as the sun set over the city. I love you. I love you, so!

Jim

[NOTE: On the envelope is written, "Forgot – also, malaria."]

Letter #21 - July 9, 1984

My dearest Lynn,

My lover...I long to be with you, so terribly. At the
Dignity service, so many there are with their lovers. I envy
them, so! I've just woken. The thought that for three weeks,
I'll awake beside you! It makes me so happy! And, of course,
I'll start each day by smothering you with kisses.

The nurse wouldn't give me the shot until I talked with a
doctor. Fortunately, wise nurse, she put me in touch with the
head of epidemiology at the University of Rochester hospital,
who also is head of the AIDS task force, here. I leveled with
him, told him my lover of seven years had become a hep carrier
and would be visiting me. His advice on our lovemaking was,
"There's no reason why you can't have a sexual relationship.
There are many safe things you can do, if you just think about
it." As for saliva being a transmitter, his comment was, "Nah!"
So, maybe you've been foregoing your favorite hobby for no good
reason. Check, again. William Valenti, MD, head of
epidemiology at U. of R. Medical Center, says nah. The exchange
of blood, feces, and semen are the dangerous things. Most
dangerous is if I am the passive partner in anal intercourse,
which we know I'm not. But I didn't ask him about greasy
fingers in my ass. I'll check that, next time I talk to him.
Once, I did bleed, I remember. The next most dangerous is anal
intercourse, with me the active partner. Damn! But to tell the
truth, I'd rather come facing you, kissing your mouth. I'm not
sure if anal insertion without ejaculation is dangerous, or if
it's my ejaculating that makes it dangerous.

Then, since he had the idea that I've been active for a
long time...I really doubt if I've had as many as a hundred
partners...he gave me the hep screen test; negative on antigens
and antibodies. So, my vaccination took place on Friday, the

6th. My second will be two weeks before I meet you. He says 85% test positive for antibodies one month after the second shot. It's important that I get my third shot, and he thinks it very unlikely that it will be available in India, which raises a tricky problem: how to get it to me, since it has to be refrigerated. I've been wondering, If I can't get it there, you might see if it couldn't be put on a plane in S.F. for Calcutta. What is your flight time and are there any stops? Is there provision for refrigeration? What would the cost be? Because if all else fails, maybe you could send it to me in January.

The doctor was mumbling something I didn't quite understand, that even if I did catch hep-B, the third shot might knock it out. The one thing I do not want to happen is for me to become a carrier, myself. I forgot to ask him the likelihood of that. He mumbled that if I caught it, my blood test might show markers. At that point, he was talking more to himself than to me.

But the main thing he said is that we can kiss, kiss, kiss and have a satisfying sexual relationship that is safe. So, my love, I'm ready and rarin' to go (come?).

Other things have been clarified, since my last letter. My visa has been approved. So, I leave as scheduled, assuming my tickets, bought in India, arrive. I will stay in New Delhi for the 15th, big show of Independence Day. I'll arrive in Calcutta the 16th or 17th. And, here's news...I will not be at the Ramakrishna Mission but I'll have a flat of my own in the U.S. consulate apartment complex in a very posh neighborhood of Ballygunge. So, I can put you up, there. But we will have to be discreet, because I'll also have a servant. A cook-bearer. The chances are that he'll be a he, but a heterosexual he. But think...at least we'll have uninterrupted power and air conditioning!

As for clothes, be prepared for rain; Monsoon season. No kissing at Dum Dum. Damn, damn.

Love and kisses galore,

Jim

Letter #22 – July 14, 1984

Dearest…

Happy birthday! (Today...not when you read this.) Give
yourself a big hug for me. Your letter from Washington was a
bit disturbing. The last thing I want to happen is for a rift
to open between you and Kit and Nick. But I trust that things
are patched up about your trip.

You mentioned arriving before me in Calcutta. I think it
is a good idea. There's a 9½ hours difference, during Daylight
Savings, eastern time in India. They are ahead. So, you have a
12½ times difference. When you hit Calcutta, you will have a
good case of jet lag. Now, mind you, when we are together, I
don't mind you're being in bed a lot. But I don't expect you to
be so gauche as to be sleeping. I'll try to arrive on the 16th.
But since I will arrange the trip in New Delhi, I can't tell you
what plane I'll be on. I'll be met by Company people, anyway.
The best way to find out where I'll be is the Company office.

Dr. (Mrs.) Kalya B.

Company Regional Office

Stout St.

Calcutta 001 001

Phone 50-505

I'm not sure exactly where the consulate apartment complex is.
My Bengali friends say it is not quite at the site of the U.S.
consulate. But it's in a posh downtown neighborhood.

Anyway, if all else fails to bring us together, we can
arrange to meet at the Victoria Memorial, inside the main
entrance (I hope there's just one!), between noon and 12:30 on
Friday, the 17th. If we miss, then same on the 18th, until we
meet. If we miss on Friday, it's because your body thought it
was midnight and you were asleep, or I didn't get into Calcutta.
I was thinking I could tell Sally, "You'll never believe who I

ran into in the Victoria Memorial; a fellow I met in Berkley. Remember, I took the kids on a picnic to Angel Island with another guy and his kids? Also, another picnic at Fort Mason? Yes. Him. He's touring the region. So, I invited him to stay in my apartment, etc., etc."

OR, you could tell me which hotel you would be at, and I'd contact you as soon as I arrived. That does sound the easiest. Why do the easiest things always occur to me last? I have a *Fodor's 1984.* The best hotel is the Oberoi Grand. Their second choice is Kenilworth on Little Russel St. In the "moderate to inexpensive", they list, "with character", the Fairlawn and Lytton and Kenilworth hotels. I see they <u>do</u> list the Ramakrishna Mission International Guest House. I have been told it is the <u>cleanest</u> place in all Calcutta.

I was reading a Canadian gay paper, *Body Politic.* In personals, I saw a most incredible ad for "pen pal". You won't believe his address:

Mr. Raj Patel

150B BK Mark Ave.

Calcutta 700 005

W.B. India

Isn't that incredible!? So, I'm sending him a letter, tomorrow, asking what a gay person does in Calcutta. Also, whether he knows a good gay cook bearer I can hire!

Raj is twenty-four, likes stamps, books, music, movies, wants to correspond with those about his age, "...or older". I stretched that. I told him my age. Ouch! But he might tolerate having some chai tea with me. Shall we look him up, while we're together, there?

Yes, I've been studying Bengali. My first words are for all their famous sweets: roshogolla; pantuci; raj bhog; kamla bhog; borfi. "Ami cha chai," is, "I want tea." "Ektou cha hawbey?", more polite is, "Can there be a little tea?" I've considered another request, "Ektou dushtu chele hawbey?", for, "Can there be a little naughty boy?" If that doesn't get results, "Ami chele chai...ack dushtu chele," for, "I want a boy...a naughty one."

Oh, well, if we want to proposition anyone, I think all we have to do is wink at them. That's easier. Again, the easiest occurs to me last. As you can see, I have been devoting my mind to the most fundamental questions.

Believe it or not, there's still complications with my visa. Although we have gotten word from India that our visas have been approved, the consulate in Chicago has not. We think India cabled New York, instead of Chicago consulate. You can't believe the beaurocratic red tape until you've been through it. India has not yet approved the issuance of our airline tickets yet, either. You, too, must get a visa, before you leave. Fortunately, tourist (short-term) visas are routine. India wants your foreign exchange too badly to hassle you.

Although your doctor doesn't recommend any shots, I think you should buy about ten chloroquine tablets (about $10) for malaria protection. Take one the week before you leave, and one each week, until they are gone. We are taking a combination of malaria tablets: one for wet season mosquitoes, one for dry season mosquitoes. I don't know the names or which is which. I think they are going to cost us, for the four of us, almost $500. Ouch!

Did I say where the girls are going to school? The most expensive school in India: the US Embassy School. Cost: $9,000. That's equal to the whole maintenance allowance of one Company. OUCH!! But it will be interesting for them to go to a school that is only 48% American. The other 52% are not Indian; the

Indian government forbids that. The other 52% are from all the other diplomats in New Delhi.

I do remember "Time After Time", lover, but only vaguely. I couldn't remember the words. I'll wait for you to teach it to me. I do know what I want from you, time after time. But I think the song must be about other things. I remember it as a melancholy tune.

When your boys were eyeing the Georgetown foxes, you may have noticed the bar across from the Georgetown Inn. An old gay bar where I met Dave Jones, the Meals-On-Wheels man in S.F. You talked to him once on the phone to invite him to my birthday party. He'd had bone cancer and two heart attacks. I'd be very surprised, but pleased, if he were still alive.

I've never been to Williamstown. Someday, we'll tour it, together. Do you think that might come true? I do hope you had a serene, beatific, birthday. I'm prepared to receive God's love through you, Lynn, my dearest. But I better stop, before I start to cry, too!

Sweet kisses all over your eyes, mouth, ears, neck, etc., on down…

Jim

Letter #23 – July 23, 1984

Dearest Lynn,

Forgive me, lover. I've been pining away for a week without hearing from you. Then, two letters, today! Now, I realize it's me that hasn't written in a week!

Zinc, you say! I'll start right away. I thought zinc was for spleen and liver. When I got mono, the doctor prescribed zinc. The other doctor who was present asked why. My doctor just smiled and said nothing very intelligible. I understand, now. Since I was about to spend the next five weeks in bed, he wanted to make sure I had something to play with, and ensured my toy was in good working order.

Don't bother buying, *Nocturnes for the King of Naples*. I'll send you my copy, which is water stained because my car trunk leaked during a rain, while I was driving here. I'll send you two or three other "serious" gay fiction I have. I thought of taking them to India. I bet Mister Navjot D. can't get his hands on things like that (not to mention Colt calendars, etc.). But I want to send you my *Nocturnes*. So, I'll send you the rest. Currently, I'm reading, *Saul's Book*. Very powerful but not beautiful like, *Nocturnes*. I may send that one to my brother, Richard, in Milwaukee, since he was the one who put me on to *Nocturnes*.

If you do look up Dave Jones, please send him my love. (No – don't be jealous. You know there's no reason to be.) The best contact would be Meals on Wheels in S.F. He always had an unlisted home phone.

Your doctor on polio. My doctor was surprised, too, when I suggested it. I got it from a State Department manual. My doctor gave it to me because it's so cheap and won't do no harm. And yes, typhoid shots are miserable. I ached and had fever.

Am I taking a hat??? Have you ever seen me in a hat? Do I own a hat? No. In fact, I am carrying so many books...I don't trust the libraries, there...that I am short-changing on my clothes. I expect to buy a lot, there. I'll have a suit in silk, hand-tailored for me. How's that?!

And don't worry about the big "F". I love you. If you wear your purple caftan with the quadruple strand of popits about your neck and go flaming down Chowinghee (Main Street), I'll be right beside you with your arm around mine. I remember your writing about Nicky nagging you not to be so flaming in the grocery store. Flame, baby, flame! You will find Bengali men sort of feminine. They are small build; they have to swish a little to keep their sandals from falling off. And the one overwhelming person in their lives is and always has been their mother. Did you know that two-thirds of the population of Calcutta is male? But since marriages are arranged by mama, most are married. They see their wives when they go on vacation.

Speaking of Mama, I can't believe you came out to Mama, because of me! Wow! What a scene. Next time you see her, give my mother-in-law a big kiss for me.

Oh, my cock always starts aching when I write to you. I haven't j.o.'d since...when?...two days ago. I may go to baths, tonight. All I do (I promise) is watch the video. I am addicted to video porn. I don't care if it's repetitive. I dig it! I get hard and stay hard for two hours straight. I like to caress my cock through the towel, just casually, gently fingering as I watch the handsome, horny dudes squirting all over each other. Sometimes, the desire to come gets close to unbearable. But that's the best; I just feel the unbearability of not coming, and on and on like that, for about two hours. It's not a bad buy for $5. I avoid the orgy room. Once, I went in there to come and sat down on the mats. A few days later, I noticed two black dots at the base of some pubic hairs. I scraped them off. I'm pretty sure they were stray crabs. I've forgotten the name of the bottle of liquid to get rid of them. I don't relish going into a pharmacy and asking, "Whatcha got for crabs...you know, pubic region, body lice.?" Last time I did that (ten years ago...I let it get out of hand), I got quite the stare. Anyway, I inspect myself, carefully. Nothing except that once. Bombay hotels:

Deluxe - Taj Mahal Intercontinental (you may want at least to visit it. The "Old Taj" part remains in its Victorian-Saracenic grandeur;

Oberoi Towers - fabulous fifth floor garden terraces and barbecue;

First Class - President on Cuffe Parade;

Nataraja on Marine Drive;

Farijas "25 off" Apollo Bunder Road, whatever that means;

Moderate, "less fancy but adequate", Bombay International, Marine Drive;

Grand, Ballard Estate;

Sea Green, Marine Drive;

Sea Palace, Strand Road-West End;

Marine Lines;

Apollo and Diplomat, both inexpensive and reasonable;

Very basic - Ascot, Astoria, Sea Green South, on Marine Drive;

Fernandes Guest House, Ballard Pier..."small but clean and inexpensive".

For touring:

Prince of Wales Museum – there's a large collection of jade, crystal, china, lacquer, and metal objects, both ancient and modern, and lots more;

Adjoining is Jehangir Art Gallery. How's this..."Many of the intellectuals of Bombay pass their time in the Samovar Café in the Jehangir Art Gallery,";

There are rock carvings from the second to fifteenth centuries in the Kanheri Caves at Borivali (near Thana, 28 miles away). The steps connecting caves on the rocky mountain side are most interesting part of excursion. Cave number three is most outstanding of the 100 caves. Check with Maharashtra Tourist Development Corporation or Sanghi International Travels or be at Government of India Tourist Office before 8:45AM;

Also, boat trip out six miles in bay to Elephanta (monsoon may interrupt this);

Also, Gandhi house on Laburnum Road, "...memorable and dolls". Dolls?

Just one thing wrong with all this: I'll not be with you.

If you go a few hundred miles south, Goa is very interesting; Portuguese influence. You can even see the remains of St. Francis Xavier, which some pilgrim bit the toe off of, about ten years ago. No kidding. It's amazing what religious fervor can make you do. The only nude beaches in India are there. But it's mostly westerners getting their buns burned, I hear.

When Ivy said you should visit Visakhapatnam, she didn't tell you it's half way down the coast to the tip of India. However, along the way are those beaches where we'll have to be constantly saved by our lifeguards. The erotic statues of Konark temple, Lake Chilika – largest lake in India. ARE YOU SURE YOUR UNION ISN'T GOING TO CALL A STRIKE? YOUR SCHOOL

DISTRICT SAVE FUNDS BY DELAYING OPENING? HOW'S YOUR SICK LEAVE?
PERSONAL DAYS? MILITARY LEAVE?

Why a Hindi-English dictionary? In Bombay, they speak
Maharashtrian. In Calcutta, they speak Bengali. But maybe she
knows something I don't.

Lover, I'm counting days; counting from today, Monday. In
three weeks and three days, we will be in each other's arms for
two weeks and three days (if you have to be back by the 4th).
Maybe...I just realized, if you go to Hong Kong, it's less time
for us. But that's SELFISH OF ME. If you spend that much
money, by all means, take in Hong Kong. Just don't take too
long. Remember, it's a small place.

Seriously, I have heard that you can save hundreds by
buying return tickets in India. BUT BE SURE before you leave.
With all the different tours and deals, you may still get the
best deal, right here. Also, buying tickets in India can be a
hassle.

I want to be drained by you, just you, nobody else but
you...boop boop de doup. Pass me the zinc, Zeke! I'm taking it
off, Jake. Shit. I can't wait.

Jim

Letter #24 – July 25, 1984

My love,

Of course, use my name. I don't have an address for myself, yet. But you could put down the Company address I gave you. (Changed pens.) That's better. Green (ink) on yellow (paper) seems bilious.

> Jim Johnson
>
> c/o Company Regional Office
>
> Stout St.
>
> Calcutta 700 017

I promise to maintain you, while in India. But if you can't repatriate yourself, tough luck. You'll just have to stay with me for the whole year.

But there must be thousands of tourists who get visas without knowing anyone in India. Ask if it's essential that it be filled in. Because you'll be in India, even before me.

It's morning. I just woke up. As I woke up, I turned around and found you still asleep, facing away. So, I kissed your neck and ear and you turned toward me and we embraced. I kissed each of your eyes, still closed. I kissed away the sleep. Then, your mouth and your throat. You grasped both our cocks together, still greasy from the night before. As we kissed and undulated, my cook comes in with our morning tea. It's obvious by now that he always knows when we're doing it, and always finds an excuse to come in. But it's OK, because he is gay. So, we thank him and ask him to bring us some more mustard oil. When he comes back, he catches me with your cock in my mouth. So, he hands you the oil, and I feel your cock go rock hard in my mouth. I wonder what's up. Ah, so that's it. You've got the cook by his balls. "Fuck your master," I hear you say. I am rather vulnerable, as I crouch over your cock. You reach up and oil my ass and his cock...Page 3. Gee, I

wonder what happened to page 2? It was a great story. Sorry
you missed out on the ending.

Good news. My visa is finally going to be issued, this
Friday. See, it took your prayers to do it. You need to pray
for one more thing: the Indian Ministry of Education has to
approve American Express' purchase of my flight tickets, which
they haven't done, yet. No approve, no tickee.

I asked my Bengali tutor about jack fruit. He doesn't
like the sweet, ripe kind. But the green is good, when cooked.
He doesn't recognize "custard apple" under that name. Ask Ivy
for its Bengali name. He recommends "wood apple", a fruit with
a hard shell. Inside, you scoop out the seeds and eat the rest.
When we sip the juice from coconuts, we should ask the coconut
wallah to slice it all the way open. The coconut is so soft,
you can scoop it out with a piece of the shell. Ask Ivy which
of these she likes: rosogolla; rajbhog; pantira; sandesh; kamala
bhog; burfi; pears; ladoo; shingara. These are famous Bengali
sweets...except, I forgot, shingara may be salty.

Two weeks...whoops, wishful thinking...three weeks, one
day, and still counting 'til heaven.

Jim

Letter #25 - July 27, 1984

Dearest...

I just got your letter, about letters, and I agree completely. We chat and be near each other through our letters. It doesn't matter if we have no news. When I was in Kalamazoo, I'll admit to a certain "fear"...that if we wrote too often, the secretary and faculty...everyone joins in distributing the departments' mail into our boxes...would begin to wonder...perhaps to peek. So, infrequency relieved my "fears". I know you'll lecture me about being at peace. But that's the way it was. And I guess you suspected as much.

But now is different. I long for your letters, as my second-to-last one said. And I apologize, again, for not flooding your box with letters. Even in the past, I could have written you and been frank with you not to write to me too frequently. But now, I remember there was another thing. I wanted you to fall in love with a local guy; someone you could do more than write letters to and remember. But you've had seven years to do that. Time's up!

I do have some news. Right this minute, Sally is in Chicago, picking up our passports, I HOPE. At least everything has been approved, by the consulate's own admission. Furthermore, my flight tickets have been approved and I should soon be getting them in the mail. But is everything approved? NO! Of all things, they haven't yet approved Sally's flight tickets. THEY'RE INSANE!

I'm so glad you're doing Hong Kong, first. I begrudge you all the days we can be together and aren't. I also am jealous of your being in Calcutta for four days without me. You're not allowed to do anything interesting! Actually, maybe you could hire a gay cook for me.

I'm sitting outside by the postbox, writing. It's a gray, cool day. But the legs and other things protruding from the shorts that pass by make up for it. I went to the baths, last night. Three-hour erection with brief intervals of rest, as cassettes changed. I love you, Lynn, and that's why I don't look at any of the guys who are there, in person. (Well, just one or two, I only look.) There were times I was sorely tempted to find a smooth and juicy suck. But somehow, it doesn't matter. It's you I want to be with. When you've got the real thing...the quick, anonymous hello/goodbye forever kind of sex just isn't very important.

Back to Calcutta...

If you want to go to the museums without me, please do. I've decided that they are no longer high on my agenda of worthwhile activities. Except, when they're small and united by a single theme. Which reminds me...your praise of the Greek revival and Georgian houses made me think I have yet to "do" Rochester. There is the George Eastman house (founder of Kodak) and the Sloan house, home of an eccentric, rich woman who collected thousands, tens of thousands, of dolls. I'll check it out. The campus, here, is quite nice. Their carillon above the library is the most musical I've ever heard. University of Rochester is overshadowed by the Ivy League which surrounds it. But it is a first-class university, nonetheless. And I'm getting a lot of studying done.

By the time this letter reaches you, you'll only have a week before you leave! My God! But it will be two weeks, three days before I see you. That's our blackout time. We'll have to make up for it during the next week.

A black guy just passed me with a Walkman over his ears. I said, "Hello, professor." Is he the same black with Walkman who, sitting on a step, whispered, "Fag," last night, as I walked into the baths? Probably not.

    'Til tomorrow, lover.

    Jim

Letter #26 - July 30, 1984

You didn't tell me how much zinc to take! Anyway, I've been
consulting vitamin and mineral books. They don't connect zinc
with profuse squirting. But I've come across a prescription
item described as "horny juice", in Durk Pearson and Sandy
Shaw's, *Life Extension*; Warner Books. It is p-acetamidobenzoate
salt of dimethylaminoethanol. Its prescription trade name is,
"Deaner", a product of Riker. Besides being "horny juice", it
is supposed to counteract some of the effects of aging, like the
accumulation of pigments in skin (liver spots) and in brain
cells. Perhaps your doctor will write a prescription, up to 300
mg per dose, for it? I bought a high zinc vitamin pill, with
other things mixed in, anyway. No noticeable effect, yet. I'm
still as horny as ever. Zinc is good for preventing dandruff
and hair loss (page 471 of book)!

Saturday - beddy time

Now I know why I took zinc during my mono! Except my hair
did fall out a lot, from the continuous fever. Or, maybe zinc
makes your hair fall out. Oh, what the hell. I've been
perusing my suitemate's copy of *Penthouse*. Isn't it a wonderful
lesbian mag? Now, if the ordinary American male could turn on
to gay male sex as much as he is apparently turned on by women
teasing each other's boobs and tonguing each other's pussies and
assholes, I'd say we were in a liberated world. I thought the
lesbian scenes well done, even loving.

I still haven't rapped up my books to send you. Will do,
tomorrow. Maybe I can get in an hour more on *Saul's Book*, by
Paul Rogers. Very gripping. But first, it's time for my super
vitamin with zinc; yuck.

Sunday - evening.

Just back from supper with Dignity group. I tried to pick
something not too caloric, dearest. But how was I supposed to

know a salad with a side order of chicken wings would be a salad plate twice the size of any other salad plate and there were a full dozen chicken wings swimming in barbecue sauce? Tomorrow, it's dinner at a colleague's parents' house. A Jewish mama but I don't think it'll be just chicken soup. You know, it's impolite not to have a second helping of chocolate cake. Then, Tuesday is our ethnic restaurant night; German, this time. For Wednesday, I've invited my Bengali tutor out to supper. I hope you don't mind if I'm ten pounds heavier than when you last saw me. You could pretend it's all muscle. Hope you have a good imagination.

I donated one of my gay novels to Dignity. It was a bulky hardcover about God's grace throwing two gays together for their own good. I thought it was a natural for their library. And it's not really as good as *Nocturne...*, or *Saul's Book*, which I'm reading, now. It was called, *In Such Dark Places*, by Caldwell.

It occurred to me that if you are in India so long before me, I won't be there to protect you from "Delhi-belly". You MUSTN'T eat your salads. Any uncooked leaf that grows near the soil, that means lettuce, celery, etc., you cannot eat. You mustn't eat any fruits or veggies without first peeling; bananas, OK. Peaches, plums, cucumbers, nix until I get there. We can soak them in a solution. Do not buy even cooked foods from street vendors. The shops are the places to buy. Yogurt is good. Ice cream at Kwality is good. For drinking, bottled liquids. Try beer; the wine is either nonexistent or "yuck". To drink the water, have it at a boil for at least ten minutes. Don't trust the tablets. Try to enjoy Indian vegetarian meals. They are always well cooked and well balanced, too. I don't want our precious few days ruined by sickness.

And behave yourself.

Don't I sound like an old scold, as if I've lived all my life, there? With all the advice I've received, it feels like it.

How are we going to fit all the side trips in? I see three: to Darjeeling; to Agra; south to Konark; etc. I don't know how much of my time will be committed to Jadavpur. My guess...I'll be largely on my own during my first two weeks. But we should be prepared psychologically if it ain't so.

Well, I said my goodbyes to the Dignity folks. A real nice bunch. Never got to sleep with the big Italian, although we have kissed. It's interesting...all the priests have been young and cute. I am amazed how different church services are from when I was growing up. They are so "down home", even folksy. Today, a nun read the gospel and gave the homily; the kingdom of God is within us. Really excellent. Shall we go to church together, in Calcutta? I'll check if there's a Methodist church. Yes, American Methodist...Methodist church on Sudder Street.

I haven't felt like this since I was a kid counting the days until a vacation trip. I am asked if I'm excited about going to India. I say, "To India? Oh, yeah, that's the place where I'll be reunited with my lover." The whole excitement, now, is in being reunited with you. Everything else is stage setting. And I'm already feeling the loss when you leave!! How's that for anticipation?

Word is, our visas are in hand. Still no word on Sally's plane ticket, yet.

Are you going to know your hotel, before you leave? If so, don't forget to tell me. If not, 12 to 12:30 Victoria Memorial, Friday. Except, if I arrive on Thursday, how can I sleep knowing you are there somewhere, only to be found the next day?

Every morning I wake up, I imagine you next to me. By the time I finish imagining you next to me, I'm oozing, dripping. But it's no use. I haven't emptied my bladder, yet. Please remember! Before we start in the morning, we first empty our bladders! See how I think of everything?

I'm now going to take a walk in the dark, so that this letter will be picked up at 6:30AM, to speed off to you. If you don't get this letter, you'll know I've been mugged. Ah, logic.

I forgot. Oh, the hell with it. You're an experienced traveler. I'm not going to give you any more advice.

Dearest, I want you to look in the mirror, give yourself a wink, and a big smile, and tell yourself, "Hi, handsome. Someone is desperately in love with you. He loves your hair, your beautiful eyes, your five o'clock shadow, and those luscious lips, whether they're smiling or kissing. He loves the you inside for your upbeat and joyous attitude toward life."

Remember to say that in the mirror.

'Til tomorrow –

Jim

Letter #27 - July 31, 1984

Dear Love,

Your picture is in front of me. Your beautiful smile I remember, so well. I don't think you've changed at all. Every morning now, I fantasize about making love to you. Even now, I've got one hand on my hard cock. You're giving me satyriasis. Thank God there's no vaccine against that.

Last night at supper (where I pigged out on pig...I mean pork), they were talking about the *Tin Drum*, too. I must read the book. I saw, "Night of Shooting Stars". I liked everything, except the stuck-on narration to the baby in the bedroom; a typical Italian sentimentality. But the movie was powerful.

Don't talk to me about paying me. I don't charge room and board to my lover...or to anyone else, for that matter. For other expenses, I'd say count on there being half what you'd pay in the states. For railroad fares, there's an excellent article in the June *National Geographic* on India's railroads. I remember they mentioned fares, which are ridiculously low. But we may have to fly to Darjeeling.

Thanks for the safety tips. You see we're thinking the same things, since I sent you the same tips a few days ago.

Your card about Navjot came yesterday, too. Since I know nothing about him, really, it's hard to say whether he can or would put you up. I wrote to him and said if he received my note by the 26th, he could write to me. Mail takes a minimum of eight days and usually ten to -? days. If I do receive a letter from him before you leave, I'll call you and let you know what to expect. All I wrote was that I'd be there and what does a gay person do in Calcutta? I'm such a trusting soul. I told him that I'd be teaching philosophy at Jadavpur University. I also suggested that we meet and have a cup of tea. I even asked if he knew of any gay cook-bearer I could hire. Since there is this 22-year gap in our ages, I can't be sure if he'll respond. I also said I'd save stamps for his collection. And guess whose envelopes are giving me an extensive collection?

Why don't you write, yourself? Introduce yourself and say you may try to look him up and hope he won't mind. There's no time...come to think of it, you'll beat that letter across the Pacific. If you haven't already done it, forget it. He says he likes music and books. Invite him to a concert and tell him you're a librarian. He also likes travel. He has a university degree. But who knows? My guess is he's very closeted. India is a prudish country. They are still very Victorian.

Today, my airline tickets came. Sally's arrived, yesterday. So now, EVERYTHING is done. I start my malaria pills, today. Alice vomited them up. I don't know what we're going to do about her.

And now, sweetest, I'm going to finish jacking off, while looking at your picture.

Love,

Jim

-Ohsogood-

Letter #28 - July 31, 1984 (second letter with this date)

Hi, again.

I'm just back from my walk, mailing your letter. I wasn't mugged. But the black guy I followed sure was worried whether I was going to mug him!

I was about to wrap the books but I haven't read all the sci fi. So, I read one story. Now, I see another I want to read. So, I wrap, tomorrow. I thought of your readings in the library when I read, *Black Rose and White Rose*. Do your kids like fairy tales? You might try that one.

1:20AM...Monday, now Tuesday...

Back from dinner at a colleague's parents. Just got off the phone; over an hour talking to my brother. Richard's in Milwaukee. He wants to visit me in India, too, at Christmas. I told him you were going to visit me. Did you know he's "one of us", as they say in Dignity, "a member of the community"? But he's much more interested in music than in sex, especially since his lover of many years deserted him for the wilds of S.F.

I haven't had time to read the sci fi. So, I still haven't wrapped books, yet.

And oh, how could I forget? I'm going to try those feathers on...yes, they're just right for brushing my nipples, a little too delicate for penile stimulation. Not bad under my ears, either. Shall we become feather fetishists?

Richard, if he comes, could carry my third shot of hep-B vax. So, problem would be solved.

I'm exhausted. Tonight, I'll sleep with you, after all, overdressed as you are; your feathers brushing my lips, getting up my nose, poking my eyes, caught in my teeth.

I just tried squeezing my cock between the card. Not quite the same as fucking you, though.

So, I'll try sleep.

-Tuesday morning-

Good morning, lover. I haven't emptied my bladder, yet.
But we made love, anyway. Do you think George Lucas named Hands
Solo after a certain act?

That vitamin book I mentioned...the authors say they are
exploring alternative nonreproductive sexual options. Their
heroes are Nureyev, Billy Jean King, Nijinsky, etc. Their
favorite sculpture is Donatello's David, Michelangelo's Bacchus
and Dying Slave. Now, I wonder what all that means?

Wow, am I excited! I just proved a little theorem which
completes a little gem of a paper that I just tossed off, last
Thursday. The quickest good paper I've written. (I can write
junk faster.) I use the word processing programs here and their
fantastic laser printer. It was the fun of that and the
encouragement of a colleague (one with parents here) that led me
to type it up. In other circumstances, I wouldn't have
bothered. I feel confident it will find a publisher.

Love,

Jim

Letter #29 – August 3, 1984

Bon Voyage! Enjoy Hong Kong. I am writing this in the lobby of the medical center. Time for my gamma globulin and second hep-B vax. Then, I do some last-minute shopping for such esoterica as swimming goggles that fit. Then, off to Groton on Hudson, where my youngest brother lives. He gets my car. Then, back here by bus; seven-hour trip, on Sunday.

Now, I'm in the room for shots. Nurse checking whether gamma globulin interferes with the hep-B vax.

So, I guess it's Victoria Memorial, 12 to 12:30, Friday; if not Friday, then Saturday. I will do what I can possibly do to be there on Friday.

Verdict is: postpone gamma globulin.

Back from shopping spree. Just called Dr. William Valenti. He says no interference between gamma globulin and hep-B. So, I pay for an unnecessary extra office bill.

A wild thing just happened. I tried to call to make another appointment and the phone is still connected to Valenti; I can hear him talking to someone else about doses of ampicillin! Dialing or yelling into phone is no good! We're hooked forever to Valenti!

He also said that my immunity chances rise from about 50 to 60%, two weeks after this shot, to 80 to 90%, four weeks after. Time of third shot not critical. If I do get hep-B, the course of disease will be altered. It's possible I might not show symptoms.

As for you, fears about how to dress, look, etc.: forget it. As Mr. Rogers used to say, "I like you as you are!" I did get a haircut, but I remembered you didn't want it short. So, it's not short.

Now, I go to the post office and off to my brother's.

Lynn, you're marvelous! I haven't been able to locate a copy of "Spartacus", anywhere!

Now, I'll read your letter.

OK, Y.M. If you're not in the foyer or entry way, I'll look for you across from the Tata Center!

No letter from Navjot, yet.

Until we meet again...arrivaderci, my love.

Jim

The First Days in Calcutta
Age 50

~~~~~

At long last, the reunion. It was 1984.

There had been weeks of letters and planning. We would meet at the Victoria Memorial in Calcutta, India, the long-distant city where Jim would be working. Wakeful hours, packing and unpacking; must have the perfect outfits. Little did I really know about the sub-continent's monsoons!

The long flight to the Crown Colony of Hong Kong ended in a terrifying landing on a tiny runway. I registered at the Hotel Fortuna in the New Territories. There were many rides on the ten-cent Star Ferry back and forth to the Manhattan-sized island. Beautiful harbor-sitting on an ancient Chinese junk; an entire world rocking on the water! A hovercraft to Macao; beauty all around.

Finally, arrival in Calcutta! There was an unforgettable jitney trip into town that found me joggled from one side of the bus to the other; a Kipling-esque, sarong-clad boy atop an elephant, and a pool with a waterfall complete with water buffalo.

I checked in at the Oberoi Grand---grand indeed!---a marble bathroom, but very dicey when the windowless room suddenly went dark while I was shaving!

So began three days on my own.

I found a tailor and ordered a white safari-style jacket, located the memorial and determined the best place to see the road and his arrival.

Time was now kaleidoscopic. India is color, heat, rain, business, rickshaws, cows, and massive, white-shirted men. The "White Marble Palace" is indeed just that, with nature slowly covering all; ancient palanquins,* peacocks, and a strolling maharajah. A visit to the mysterious Jain Temple, then a cinema seating hundreds of men, showing a film history of British rule from the Indian point of view, (much disdainful muttering!).

A horoscope reading in the hotel lasted several hours. The subjects of House of Astrology's Chatterjee Mukand's advice and observations included: "look to your mother's health**; family peace; children's studies come up very much; writing books could be very much successful; avoid carbohydrates." I was "honest, sincere, but stubborn," but there was not one word about my future.

. . . The day arrives . . .

* A covered litter for one passenger; a large box on two horizontal poles carried by four to six people.

** Not to worry; she lived to the age of 97.

~~~~~

Time's Up

August 16, 1984

Oberai Grand Hotel
Victoria Memorial
Calcutta, India

~~~~~

Please, please lights stay on! I must look my best, smell delicious, be clean-shaven; no

blood!

Made it!

At fifty, I was told I looked thirty-five, and that is how I felt, anyway. My new

jacket fit just right---looking good in white!

I began the first of a dozen time checks, using the very watch my parents had

given me for my high school graduation. Ironic! If Mother had known why I was using

it on this day, thirty years after our breakfast-room showdown, she just might have

found "The Answer," herself.

A quick bite in the Oberoi dining room. I can't remember what I ate or how I got

to the Victoria Memorial. Strange looks followed me, perhaps because my feet were not

touching the ground.

The Victoria Memorial---a large white-domed building built soon after the old queen died in 1901; well-laid-out grounds, a wide path leading to the street. I was greeted by an ancient, white-headed fellow who must have come with the building in '01!

We planned to meet in the foyer, but I wanted a better long view to the street, so I ran up the stairs. I was early, all the better to be composed. The window framed the grounds, path, and the street fifty yards away.

So, I began my watch and watch-checking; exactly at noon. How was he coming? I assumed by car. Traffic was light; when a car did stop, I would lean forward. A person might get out, but not Jim; I knew that walk, or if were me, run. No one appeared on the path; no cars stopped. It was 12:15; not to worry. But by 12:30, then 1:00, worry set in. I became that parent again. Where? Why?

Casual meet-ups are one thing, but, dear Tracker, once you have read the letters---wild horses!!

By two of the clock, I was frantic. How I got down those stairs and moved I can't tell you.

I had the company office address in my wallet; on Short Street. Perhaps they knew what had happened; where he was.

I asked a well set-up man if he knew Short Street. He did and would walk me there. Minutes later, we arrived and he pointed. Before I could thank him, he looked me straight in the eye and asked, "Am I dismissed?" I was appalled. (Was it two-hundred years of British exploitation speaking)? I stammered thank you, but no more. I moved stiffly to the entrance. The fresh clean rain of the morning was gone. I was sweaty, hair matted; my jacket dusty and just as wilted as I was.

Once inside, I was greeted by a sari-clad woman sitting at a desk. (In 1984, Indian women kept to that beautiful dress). "I'm looking for Dr. Flanders," I said. She half-smiled and motioned to the door to her left. "He is with Dr. Gupta," she said.

I had mixed emotions. He was all right, but where was he three hours ago?

I asked for paper and wrote the two words that meant so much---to me, at least: "Time's up."

I began to slowly back up, stopping only when I hit the wall.

When that door opened, there was once again a framing---but six years later.

What I saw was startling. He was recognizable, but somehow, he seemed shorter, diminished. He came toward me with a nervous smile. Hunching over, he offered a pathetic embrace of me against the cold wall.

"Where were you?"

. . . Forgive me when I now offer you low lights of the following two days. First, nothing physical took place after the hug. I was introduced at his lodging as a friend who was going to "crash," (he had that right!) at his apartment.

For the life of me, I can't remember the "why." I do remember the last bit . . .

"and by that time, it was too late, you were on your way." Panic turned to numbness.

New plane tickets arranged; two days home. Low lights of those hours: rickshaw ride; no hand-holding; walking together like two zombies in the street when an old man dropped dead in front of us, bubbles coming out of his mouth.

I started to stop to do something---who knows what---when Jim said, "Come on." We walked around him. I feel ashamed to this day, but remember I did share a bedroom with Rex Arthur; I follow. . . .

That last night, we were lying side-by-side, flat on our backs, a canyon between us. Finding my thoughts and voice, I asked, "So why did you wait until I had flown half-way around the world before . . ." Before I could utter one more word, he began sobbing; the bed shook. It was a heart-breaking sound for both of us.

Somehow, I knew at that moment I could not hate him. Fear had won; it had smothered that other emotion. We all know that name.

The last time I saw him was at the airport as I climbed the steps to the plane door. Now, I was the one framed. I looked back. He placed his palms together and bowed. I needn't have looked at my watch; time had stopped.

Thirteen years later, I sent him a Christmas card. Read on.

~~~~~

Letter #30 – February 3, 1998

Dear Lynn,

What a delightful surprise to return to school and find your Christmas card! I won't assume you have forgiven me, but at least I need not be afraid of your wrath any longer, is that right? It took me a month to write back, partly because of work; I am teaching a course that has 180 students in it and I am revising the syllabus, this term. Also, my graduate level course has two other profs sitting in (!), and partly because I have enjoyed writing and rewriting in my head what I would finally put down on paper. But the time to write is now, perhaps because of the proximity to February 14th, which you should not read much into, but not nothing, either. I have over the thirteen years since we last met, thought about you, wondered how you are, whether you have fallen in love and found Shangri La. Your card has been the basis of renewed speculation. Here is what I have come up with...

You have taken early retirement and moved to the Carolinas to be near your grandchildren. Your first son is still in the military, I'd bet, and he is stationed nearby. Your other son is a computer whiz with a job in the triangle cities in North Carolina. Both have kids; you're a grandpa, four times over. Perhaps you have moved there, also, with your lover, or did you leave your heart in San Francisco? You have joined a choral group and are seriously considering studying to become a gourmet chef. End of fortune cookie, and I suppose about as accurate.

So, you will have to tell me the real story about yourself over the last thirteen years. As for me, you can tell a lot about me, already. Still in the same job, and not contemplating retirement for several more years. Still in the same house, still married, no grandchildren yet, and only one son-in-law. Back in 1985, while still in India, I told Sally all, and she took it really hard, but eventually, she decided she did not want a divorce. A few years later, when I was misdiagnosed with liver cancer until they discovered it was only a cyst on my liver and an overzealous interpretation of some blood results, she decided she really did love me, anyway, despite my limitations. And I love her. We are friends and good companions.

The cause of my telling her in India was the Indian boy whose ad I had answered, while in the states. I believe I told you about him. I developed such a passion for him that it was overwhelming. We've been together, ever since. Sally consented to being a co-sponsor for his coming to the United States, and he wouldn't consider coming, unless I stayed with her. So, something like the movie, "Dona Erlinda's Son". Currently, he has just finished his doctorate in English at Michigan State, and is looking for a teaching job. His dissertation was on Tennessee Williams. Over the years, we have had rocky times, but the original passion was strong enough to weather it all. In those years, I have only had two serious competitors: a Belgian millionaire lawyer who visited him, and a varsity quarterback! Well, you don't have to believe me; I certainly wouldn't, if someone told me this. Apparently, what I had going for me is simply our compatible tastes in literature, culture, music, and a willingness to read and discuss what he has written, and not just gratitude and reverence for old age.

Agh! I am pushing sixty. And you're there, already. But I can't imagine that fact getting you down. You bubble over with enthusiasm. I am not bald or totally silvery, yet. My weight is 188...I was ten to fifteen pounds lighter, when you knew me. I used to be six feet, but I am shrinking and the shrinking is accelerating, I am afraid. Every year or so, my spine goes into some major resettling. Old age ain't for sissies. (But I *am* a sissy! Whaaaah!) Write to me about your last dozen years. If you want, I have an email address...

Affectionately,

Jim

Letter #31 - July 12, 2000

Dear Lynn,

Procrastination wins, again. So, here's hoping your Bastille Day celebration <u>was</u> fun, since I'm sure this arrives late.

I've been in Canada at Niagara on the Lake, watching British plays and developing a renewed appreciation for the emotionality of American plays. How could the British like all that cerebral speechifying? Anyway, enough G.B. Shaw and Noel Coward. I'm ready for Tennessee Williams.

The news from here is absolutely no news. The only thing to happen is my Indian boy (40-year-old boy) has finally put enough miles between us to keep me at bay. He has a tenure track job, teaching English in Seattle. So, the news is that I'm surviving. I have not yet turned inwardly into a corpse, as I thought I would.

I just sent off my registration for a two-week trip to China in October, with a bunch of philosophers. I'm not enthusiastic about it. It was more like, "What the hell, why not?" (Why not a stopover in Seattle, I say to myself.) Maybe I am a bit depressed.

Enough of that. I can see you bubbling over with fun and laughter, as you work on your theater, winning applause and prize...happy with your lover. I know you've invited me for a visit and one of these days, I'll get in my car and say, "What the hell, why not?"

Love,

Jim

Letter #32 – March 25, 2002

Dear Lynn,

I know...two years since I last wrote; you probably have wondered whether I was dead. It's felt that way, sometimes. In fact, now I cannot sit comfortably. If I do, I get a stabbing pain in my sacroiliac joint that is an eleven on a scale of one to ten.

It's been an awful time. Two deaths. My father was diagnosed with lung cancer in the same week my mother broke her hip. I was on a sabbatical that Fall, so I spent two months in Florida with them. Six months later, I was down there again, just in time to take my father to the hospital for the last time. That was last May. My mother recovered and is walking with a walker.

The real shocker was my next younger brother. He already had pancreatic cancer at the funeral but didn't know it until several months later. When the news came, I was on sabbatical, again (two separate semesters) and so, I spent two months in Milwaukee, doing whatever I could. He died November 1st, at age sixty-one. He was my gay brother. He had kept it from the family. But one of my other brothers made a point of verifying his suspicions after his death and succeeded. So, I am dealing with the shock!...shock!!...shock!!!, in the family.

All has not been awful. I made it to China for two weeks, before going to Florida and after my brother died. I went to India for two months, delivering lectures. The Indians are wonderful hosts. It was great and one school will publish my lectures as a book.

As for that Indian in my life, formerly, I seem to have been indiscreet in a letter I wrote to his therapist at his request and now, he's not communicating with me; anyway, he's in Seattle.

The invitation to visit you both is very welcome, but I just can't say when. One of my daughters has gone off to Australia and so off to Australia I go; this time, with my wife. She did not go on the China or India trips. My older daughter is a professor of history, now in Cleveland! I will be sixty-four in a few months, but the prospect of retiring is not attractive to me. I will probably hang in there until I no longer enjoy it and cease doing a good job.

Jim

Letter #33 – June 11, 2005

Dear Lynn,

Surprise, surprise! Just when you figured I must be dead or something, here I am, again.

Now putting first things first, how come you're still so gorgeous? Do you age at all??? That picture of you on your 70th is still in my mind, creating envy and lust. I can't say I have held up as well, although I was carded at a grocery store, the other day. The lady cashier asked if I qualified for any discounts. I said I was an old man. She replied that wouldn't count, because I would have to be over sixty. I shook her hand and showed her my driver's license. She insisted I didn't look sixty.

And, truth to tell, I don't feel sixty-seven. I just finished a half hour of laps at the swimming pool. I still have no need at all for Viagra. What I need is a lover! I did make up with my dear boy (now over 45) but he's in Seattle; so, it goes.

Sally and I are now retired. But I still teach! Seven "independent studies" are now in progress, one voluntary reading group, and one course scheduled for next winter. I still have an office there and receive mail, there. But I come and go as I please, skip department meetings, etc.

We are going to Paris for the whole month of September; then, on to southeastern France in October. So, my new project is learning French!

Love,

Jim

PS: I forgot to mention, I am now also a grandpa, with number two due in September, when we're in Paris. Predictions are it will be a girl, as was the first, a real darling. They are my older daughter's and they live in Cleveland.

Jim's Last Hours

———

Passing away, passing on, passing over, or just plain passing . . . as I write this adventurous remembrance, I choose not to choose one of these time-extending ways of being; rather I choose to think of Jim joyously, hurrying to my front door, carrying a ruined birthday cake.

Jim, a Catholic, had his own thoughts and feelings about what might come to pass. We'll leave it at that.

Writing as Lynn, I want to tell an imaginary story about Jim's last hours. I'll be present, as will others---his wife, daughters, grandchildren, family.

I'll either be invisible or "Who is that person"? I can't decide. The former has obvious advantages; a simpler choice. Let's, however, settle on the latter; more theatrical; I'll be non-committal; just a friend.

Either way, I would be a watcher. So, what will I see . . . a sense of loss, regret, relief, gratitude; love, of course, or a little of all of these?

Many tears there will be; mine among them. I see myself slowly moving to the bedside, looking down at the sleep-like composure of that dear face. I'll run my fingers through his hair, touch his eyes and lips.

I'll speak softly to him. "Jim, I was sick to hear you have, for years, suffered a lot

of really bad illnesses. Oh, Jim, I'm so sorry. You have loved passionately and

brilliantly, but with some choices; choices we all understand, and you fell short in one

important way; you let fear move you slowly to not remembering---not remembering

what was in front of us all the while. Yes, Jim, it was *The Answer*.

I love you.

Goodnight, sweet prince.

———

CONCLUSION - *More or Less*

———

Now is the time for our hands to slip apart. Please don't fret; the warmth will linger, as will the discoveries we made together. Trust them. They are, after all, *The Answer*.

Jim asked if I had found Shangri-La. No, Jim, I did not find that imaginary place. I found something much more real.

I found *myself*.

———

So, we have found *The Answer*. Now let us all live the question.

The following was my critique of de Maupassant's story,
"The Answer," at age nineteen.

The Answer

Guy de Maupassant

The story begins on the Mediterranean coast of France in the latter part of the last century. Because the city of Nice is the farthest point east on the French Riviera, one can assume it was here where Corsica was sited. The characters, who hear the story about the Corsican romance, are of France's lower-upper class. There is a five-year flash-back that makes up the main part of the story.

No one character is developed to any great extent. Guy de Maupassant has presented them briefly, solely to tell a story of love, pure and simple.

The old gentleman is somewhat of an explorer; an adventurer, but outside of being keenly perceptive, his character remains a mystery.

The two lovers stand more as symbols than characters of an integrated plot. The old soldier, who appears in action only, and not in words or thought, seems to keep on living because he is happy. Despite his age and deafness, there is a bond between them which only death can break. In this situation, where love has been the only contributor toward their happiness, it is probable their deaths will follow close to one another.

The plot revolves around the story of the Corsican lovers. The story is told by an old gentleman, who had some years ago discovered the island's secret and was now revealing it to his friends at a summer villa on the French Riviera.

The beginning of the story is told from the omniscient point of view, while the rest is told from the old gentleman's point of view.

Certainly, the lovers' mountain home was not the most romantic retreat they could have chosen. Rather, I imagine, it was chosen from necessity. Guy de Maupassant chose it most likely because of its bleakness and crudeness. Corsica serves as a vivid and savage backdrop for this tender love story, which despite all of its apparent drawbacks, reached a higher state of development than most continental romances. This was accomplished by two people who gave of themselves completely and without reserve. Adam and Eve most certainly had an easier task before them, for they lacked the memory of a past life. And, too, the plain-less island of Corsica, with its deep ravines and mountains, was no Garden of Eden.

The beautiful city of Florence, with its inhabitants living graciously while basking in the Mediterranean climate and enjoying the grandeur of an unparalleled cultural heritage, could scarcely boast of citizens more contented than were these two islanders. For all the cultural wealth of Europe might as well not have existed as far as they were concerned. The music which had resounded from Florence and all Italy never reached the shores of Corsica. But the life of the old couple hidden within Corsica's walls had been just as complete and happy without the creative art of man.

They had created something far more durable. It was something far more breathtaking than the Winged Victory of Samothrace. Certainly, the Venus de Milo deserves not more acclaim than they do, nor does *Pilgrim's Progress*, nor *Forever Amber*.

Look, Mr. Ethan Brand, and Mr. James Duffy, and you, too, Mr. Nikolay Kolpakov, yes, and you, Miss Marya Vassilyevna---look and see how life could have been.

———

FOUND WITHIN THE MEMOIR

———————

<u>BOOKS, STORIES</u>

A Pocket Full of Seeds (2005), Marilyn Sachs.

Days and Nights in Calcutta (A Ruminator Find) (1995), Bharati Mukherjee, Clark Blaise.

In Dark Places,(2009), Gillian Flynn. (2018,TV movie).

Life Extension: A Practical Scientific Approach (1983), Durk Pearson, Sandy Shaw.

Lord of the Second Advent; A Rare Look Inside the Terrifying World of the Moonies (1981), Steve Kemperman.

Nocturnes for the King of Naples (1978), Edmund White.

On Human Nature (1978), Edward Wilson.

Saul's Book (1983), Paul T. Rogers.

"Snow White and Rose Red", a story by the Brothers Grimm.

The Groves of Academe (1952), Mary McCarthy.

The Premier Book of Major Poets: An Anthology (1970), Anita Dore, ed.

<u>MOVIES</u>

Dona Herlinda and Her Son.

The Front Runner, 2018.

PEOPLE

Ivy - A native of Calcutta who was a child in 1948, when Gandhi
    was assassinated.

Laura Adams Armer (1874-1963) - Author, winner of Newbery Medal
    for her book, *Waterless Mountain* (1932).

Sidney Armer (1871-1962) - Artist

Patricia Nell Warren (a.k.a. Patricia Kilina (1936-2019)-
    Novelist-(*The Front Runner*), poet, editor, journalist, gay
    activist.

A Word About My Postscripts

Dear Tracker,

One postscript led to another and to another; I finally was faced with yet another choice. As you can see, I decided to include all three. If you have had enough right now, lean back, and when you are ready, take my hand one last time.

Oh my, oh my, oh my!

Thank you.

P.S.

Our story of tracks and letters are all laid out on white paper. We all know what a challenge such plain and cold paper can be – staring at us, as if to say, "Well, I'm ready; take your first step."

How easy someone else's letters make that job happen, or so it seems, whether using a Smith-Corona or the latest gift from the partially eaten apple…if that apple is, as I suspect, a Gravenstein.

My childhood backyard had the last standing Gravenstein apple tree from an old orchard. It gave us large, firm, green fruit with a juicy, tart taste all summer long; an acquired taste! One bite or word of such a taste may cause a hesitation, giving time to wipe the juice away.

The tracks are mine, complete with some bitter taste; they were chosen, as time is marked through the retrieval of memories. Some cause noticeable winces, others are of a kind that bring a rush of sweet pleasure.

But the letters, love letters, are there with margined and double-spaced perfection. Every "I" dotted and every plosive "T" crossed, all the better to write love words with lots of T's.

Give me a moment while I seek out my husband and embrace him. This experience of a past story of love is, I believe, one worth sharing, but must be always part of living the question, but not so intense as to forget that a hug and kiss in real time is to honor the all as we face each other while refining the question*.

The letters in our story have been silently waiting in a lovely hand-painted wooden box on various shelves, over the years. Little did I know that the question and answer were right there on stationery and ink. Two joyful people with it all in their grasp.

Alas, fear is the enemy, the attacker of the answer. It pries open the fingers, one by one, at painful times, leaving desperation and, finally, resignation in the empty palm; the lifeline fainter and lifeless, as years pass.

So, the passionate transcribed words, dear Tracker, are pulled from the page, click by click. But please honor dear Jim by willingly suspending disbelief and help by adding my bits, front and back, to a tale all too true. There are no false steps, only tracks that do lead to the glorious question and the eternal answer.

I always ended my podcast show by asking my guest, "What is the universal question?" Trouble answering? I'd say dig deeper. You will not be finding China; you'll be finding complete and joyous freedom.

P.P.S.

Now you have read the letters. The passion and humanity were meant, of course, for one lover writing to another. My choice to offer this memoir was my way of sharing a love story, a story I believe is worth telling.

"What would your letters to Jim have added to the story?", one might ask. In any case, I shall remain anonymous, as will Jim.

We are important only to each other. You, dear Tracker, don't need our being the quick and the dead; our story and choices may add to your grasp of the question and the answer.

P.P.P.S.

Today, as I said, the letters live in a hand-painted wood box. Lying on top of Jim's letters is a sealed envelope addressed to my granddaughter. When the box is hers, she will find her completed granddad.

The last line reads, "When you share my story, and you will, please be kind."

*What is the universal question? The answer is, "Do you love me?"

––––––––

Nocturnes for the King of Naples
A Robed Regent Reunion

———

Dear one,

I never did receive your copy of *Nocturnes for the King of Naples*, nor did I seek it out after Calcutta. Now as an old "guy," (why did I choose that word; I have never been a "guy"), but let's move on. I sit here reading that very important book to you---a used copy---signed.

My God, just when I think our time together and the letters say it all, I read page 63 of *Nocturnes*. It makes the time before Calcutta even more beautiful and the time afterward more tragic; yes, tragic---just read "The Answer." It settles any other stray feelings with half-hearted questions.

Some of us now think of the afterlife as consisting of energy. I like to think this is true, and your extraordinary energy and presence are with me right now; my tears tell me it is true.

Our love story, then, has more nocturnes.

There is a God.

———

Made in the USA
Columbia, SC
09 November 2020